TWENTIETH-CENTURY HISTORIES

The Cold War

Paul Hastings

1945-1969

LONDON · ERNEST BENN LIMITED · 1969

First published 1969 by Ernest Benn Limited
Bouverie House, Fleet Street, London, E.C.4
© R. Paul Hastings 1969
Distributed in Canada by
The General Publishing Company Limited, Toronto
Maps drawn by K. J. Wass
Book designed by Kenneth Day
Printed in Great Britain
510–17903–7

*The illustration on the title-page shows the Russian flag being
hoisted above the ruined Reichstag, over ravaged Berlin, May 1945*

CONTENTS

MAPS

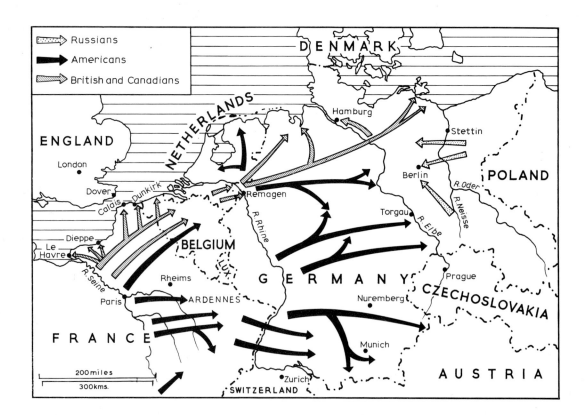

PRINCIPAL BOOKS CONSULTED

Keesing's Contemporary Archives
The Observer
The Annual Register
Encyclopaedia Britannica Year Book
The Cold War as History by L. J. Halle (Chatto & Windus)
The Hard and Bitter Peace by G. F. Hudson (Pall Mall)
The Age of Containment: The Cold War by D. Rees (Macmillan)
Ruin and Resurgence by R. C. Mowat (Blandford)
Since 1945 edited by J. L. Henderson (Methuen)
The Struggle for Europe by Chester Wilmot (Collins)
The Second World War, Vol VI: *Triumph and Tragedy* by Winston S. Churchill (Cassell)
The Development of the Communist Bloc edited by R. Pethybridge (Heath & Co.)
The Pattern of Communist Revolution by H. Seton-Watson (Methuen)
The East European Revolution by H. Seton-Watson (Methuen)
City on Leave. A History of Berlin 1945–1962 by P. Windsor (Chatto & Windus)
The Chinese Revolution by T. Mendes (Thames & Hudson)
The Birth of Communist China by C. P. Fitzgerald (Penguin)
Mao Tse Tung by S. Schram (Penguin)
Chinese Communism edited by D. N. Jacobs and H. H. Baerwald (Harper & Row)
The Communist Conquest of China by L. M. Chassin (Weidenfeld & Nicolson)
Korea: The Limited War by D. Rees (Macmillan)
Malaya: The Communist Insurgent War 1948–1960 by E. O'Ballance (Faber)
South-East Asia in Turmoil by B. Crozier (Penguin)
The Battle of Dien Bien Phu by J. Roy (Faber)
Stalin by I. Deutscher (Penguin)
Khrushchev by M. Frankland (Penguin)
The Break-up of the Soviet Empire in Eastern Europe by G. Ionescu (Penguin)
The Bitter Heritage: Vietnam and American Democracy 1941–1966 by A. M. Schlesinger Jnr. (Deutsch)
Vietnam! Vietnam! by F. Green (Penguin)
Recent History Atlas by M. Gilbert (Weidenfeld & Nicolson)

MAP NO. 1   THE FALL OF NAZI GERMANY

1 The End of the Grand Alliance

WORLD WAR II ended as it had begun in two separate stages. In Western Europe the D-Day landings of 6 June 1944 and the gradual reconquest of France foreshadowed the inevitable German defeat. As the Allies advanced from the West the Russian armies, who by May 1944 had cleared the Germans from Russian soil, poured into the German satellite states from the East. Romania was taken in August 1944. Bulgaria and Yugoslavia followed in September and October. By January 1945 Hungary too had fallen, and the Russian advance had continued into Czechoslovakia and Poland. At the close of the month the Russians crossed the German frontier and on 21 April their first shells fell on Berlin (see Map 1).

As the cellars became the permanent homes of Berliners the German front also crumbled in the West. At the end of January Hitler's last counterstroke failed in the Battle of the Ardennes. On 8 March the U.S. First Army crossed the Rhine at Remagen, and while the British and Canadian armies headed north towards Hamburg the Americans raced across central and southern Germany. On 26 April American and Russian patrols met at Torgau in central Germany. The Americans had covered 1,120 kilometres in ten months after the Normandy landings but the Red Army had won the race for Berlin.

On 23 April the first Russian detachments entered the German capital which had become 'a blazing hell' from non-stop artillery bombardment. Block by block they fought their way towards the city centre meeting fanatical resistance from S.S. battalions, Hitler Youth brigades, and the ageing veterans of Goebbels' Home Guard. While Russian infantry drove the enemy with bayonets and grenades from buildings, barricades, and the Berlin Underground, Soviet tanks crashed through the blazing, debris-littered streets. German resistance was bitter but short-lived. On 30 April, with Russian tanks half a mile from his bunker, Hitler committed suicide. Two days later Berlin capitulated. Its half-crazed defenders were barely recognisable as human beings.

> Shaggy-headed, bearded and grimy they emerged . . . from bunkers . . . tube stations and piles of ruins. Some threw their weapons away with sullen faces; others . . . stacked their rifles where they were told; many laughed hysterically . . . as they trailed through the shattered city. . . .[1]

Throughout the night they were marched to prison camps through the Brandenburg Tor, the monument beneath which German Imperial and Nazi armies had so often triumphantly passed, and the undefeated German army of 1918 had returned with flying colours to Berlin.

There was, however, to be no repetition of 1918. By 5 May all of Germany save a few small areas was in Allied hands. Hamburg was occupied by the British; the Americans held Munich and Nuremberg, the birthplaces of Nazism; while the Russian Red flag flew over the smouldering ruins of Berlin. Left without alternative the German commanders surrendered unconditionally on 7 May 1945 in the small school

[1] Keesing's Contemporary Archives, p. 7174.

1   Flanked by two
aides, General Alfred
Jodl, Hitler's brilliant
Chief of Operations,
signs the German
surrender

house at Rheims which served as the American General Eisenhower's headquarters. The war in Europe was over.

In a London bedecked with flags, hundreds of thousands of civilians and servicemen brought traffic to a standstill as they sang and danced in the streets. After nearly six years of blackout bonfires blazed, fireworks flashed, and public buildings were illuminated. 'This is your victory', Britain's war-time Prime Minister, Winston Churchill, told the cheering crowds. 'Victory in the cause of freedom in every land. In all our long history we have never seen a greater day than this. . . .'

Elsewhere the story was the same. Over a million New Yorkers blocked Broadway and Wall Street, and waded knee-deep through ticker-tape and paper streamers in Manhattan. In Moscow vast crowds danced in Red Square and staged victory demonstrations outside Allied embassies. British and American officers were embraced in the streets by jubilant Muscovites, and after dark, while Moscow's guns thundered out a great salute, searchlights and rockets lit the sky. In Paris, four years occupied by the Nazis, huge crowds marched down the Champs Elysées singing the *Marseillaise*. The British Empire and Commonwealth and other Allied countries also celebrated with enthusiasm. Only in Australia was the jubilation subdued. Here people were conscious that the conflict was not over, and that Japan, their nearest enemy, remained undefeated.

Japan's defeat promised to be a long and costly task. On 27 July she responded defiantly to an Allied ultimatum to surrender. By August plans for an invasion of Japan were complete, but they were never used. In four days Japan was crushed by the most startling events in the history of warfare.

The idea of an atomic bomb had been conceived by British scientists as early as 1939. In October 1941 British and American efforts had been combined, and British atomic scientists were despatched to work in the United States where plants were built free from the danger of German bombing. Grave anxiety was aroused by the fact that Germany, too, was engaged in nuclear research, but German progress was hampered by the destruction of large supplies of 'heavy water', necessary for making bombs, during commando raids on Norway in 1942–3. Meanwhile in America, in the closest secrecy, 95,000 workers began the manufacture of atomic bombs. They were installed with their families in the prefabricated barracks of 'atom bomb cities' in Washington and Tennessee. As they worked planes guarded the areas by day and night.

2 'V.E. Day',
Piccadilly Circus,
London

3 Hiroshima. An
Allied correspondent
stands in rubble before
what was formerly a
cinema

The fruits of their labours were reaped at 9.00 a.m. on 6 August 1945 when a lone American Superfortress dropped the first bomb upon the great Japanese port and army base of Hiroshima.

> . . . A city going about its business on a sunny morning went up in a mountain of dust-filled smoke, black at the base and towering into a plume of white to 40,000 feet. . . . Most of Hiroshima [reported Tokio Radio] no longer exists. The impact of the bomb was so terrific that practically all living things . . . were . . . seared to death. . . . Buildings were crushed. . . . Those outdoors were burned to death and those indoors killed by the indescribable pressure and heat. . . .[1]

A second bomb was destined on 9 August for Kokura. The pilot, unable to find his target in heavy cloud, dropped it instead upon the shipbuilding and armaments centre of Nagasaki which went up like an erupting volcano 'in a roar of smoke and flame' visible for over 250 miles. 'We are in possession of the most destructive weapon ever designed by man', announced American leaflets dropped over Japan.

'The force from which the sun draws its power', warned President Truman, 'has been loosed against those who brought war to the Far East. . . . If they do not accept our terms they may expect a rain of ruin from the air the like of which has never been seen on this earth. . . .'[2]

Japan needed no further prompting. 160,000 Japanese had been killed or injured at Hiroshima and 120,000 at Nagasaki. In accordance with an agreement made six months earlier Russia had also entered the war on 7 August and her troops were advancing into Manchuria and Korea. On 14 August the Japanese Cabinet surrendered unconditionally; formal documents of surrender were signed on 2 September and World War II ended completely, exactly six years after it had begun. In the capitals of the victors the carnival activities of 'V.E. Day' were repeated, while in China crowds wept for joy at the end of a war which for them had started in 1931.

[1] Keesing's Contemporary Archives, p. 7366.   [2] Ibid., p. 7368.

Now was the time to count the cost. World-wide devastation was much greater than in 1918. Technological progress in warfare and bigger battle areas made this inevitable. Civilian populations had also suffered more than in World War I because of the deliberate use of air attack to destroy civilian morale. Germany, left physically untouched in 1918, had been reduced to a wilderness. Many other Western European countries had suffered likewise. France and Holland had both been invaded and liberated within five years. Italy bore the scars of one of the bitterest campaigns of the war. Many centres of British industry had been destroyed by bombing, while the German armies in Russia had partly or completely devastated 15 large cities, 1,710 towns, and 70,000 villages. 6 million buildings had vanished, and 25 million people were homeless. In China the damage was incalculable. Of the main combatants only the U.S.A. was ✳ left with its territory and industry unscathed.

Since it had been a war of movement and machines rather than of men and fixed position, military losses for some nations were lighter than in World War I. France lost half a million lives, including those killed in the resistance movement and by air attack – only a third of her casualties in the previous war. British Commonwealth losses amounted to 445,000, over half of which came from the United Kingdom, while a further 60,000 civilians died in air raids. America, who had had over 12 million troops in the field, lost only 325,000. The defeated powers on the other hand, plus Russia and China, lost lives on a greater scale than in 1914–18. $3\frac{1}{2}$ million Germans died in battle together with 800,000 civilian personnel. Japan lost $1\frac{1}{2}$ million soldiers and half a million civilians. China's losses of soldiers and civilians in 1939–45 were 200,000 more. Russian casualties were far greater than those of any other belligerent. $7\frac{1}{2}$ million Russian soldiers died at the hands of the Germans together with $2\frac{1}{2}$ million civilians. In these grim statistics lay part of the explanation for future events.

In addition to those who had died, millions of others were homeless or else refugees in foreign lands. These presented a gigantic problem of resettlement and rehousing to the post-war world. Great administrative difficulties waited in those countries which ✗ had experienced German or Japanese occupation. Here civil service and police forces required reorganisation, resistance movements had to be disarmed, and orderly government restored. Occupation, with its division between collaborators and resistance movements, had in many countries either led to or prepared for social revolution and civil war, while in the East the Japanese overthrow of colonial régimes had quickened pre-war demands for national independence.

Overshadowing the myriad of post-war problems lay 'the Bomb'. The bomb that had destroyed Hiroshima had the blast equivalent of over 20,000 tons of high explosive, and equalled half the tonnage dropped during the entire war on Berlin. That which fell on Nagasaki was more powerful still. Not until American troops landed in Japan did they realise that great numbers had died from deadly gamma rays released at the moment of discharge or from the ghastly effects of radioactive dust. As the months passed it was found that the bombs also had dire effects upon those unborn when they were dropped. Mankind had at last produced a weapon with which it could destroy itself.

> The possibilities for good or evil [stated Sir John Anderson] are infinite. There may on the one hand be . . . fruitful development in the interests of mankind. There may on the other hand be a maniac dream of death, destruction and dissolution. . . . There are problems here calling for statesmanship of the highest order. . . .[1]

Effective control of this terrible new weapon and the future peace of the world presupposed the continuation of the wartime alliance between Britain, Russia, and the U.S.A., but there were already ominous signs that this was not to be. The Grand Alliance between Russia and the Western powers had been born of necessity and each side had delayed the union as long as possible. Past relationships between the two were clouded by mutual suspicion and distrust. Their political systems and beliefs were completely opposed. British and American troops, largely at the instigation of Winston Churchill, had been among the forces which had vainly tried to crush the Russian Communist revolution between 1918 and 1920. At the Versailles Settlement in 1919, the absent Soviet Republic was deliberately isolated from capitalist Western Europe by a barrier of states erected along its western frontiers. Excluded in this way by a re-constituted Poland, and the new republics of Finland, Estonia, Latvia, and Lithuania, established out of the western territory of Imperial Russia, the shattered Soviet Union was left to seek a solitary salvation (see Map 2).

Communism did not sweep across Europe after 1919 as the Russians had expected and the West had feared. By 1928 Russia, under Joseph Stalin, had changed its policy of 'world revolution' to that of 'Socialism in one country', and was trying to build out of the ruins of feudal Tsarist Russia a modern industrial state. Mutual hostility, however, still remained. The wave of industrial troubles throughout America and Western Europe in the twenties; the presence of Communist agents in backward countries like China; and the continuation of the Comintern, formed in 1919 to promote world revolution, all caused communism to remain a very real 'spectre haunting Europe'.

Similarly, Russia feared a repetition of the 'Intervention' attempted by the hostile capitalist West at the end of World War I. Its Communist régime remained unrecognised by America until 1933, and was not admitted to the League of Nations until 1934. The brutal enforcement of collective farming, the activities of the Russian police state, and the treason trials of the thirties did more to alienate public opinion in the West. Indeed many French and British conservative politicians saw in Nazi Germany

[1] Keesing's Contemporary Archives, p. 7368.

a valuable protective bulwark against Soviet Russia. Russia was not drawn into European politics as a counterpoise to Germany in the middle thirties as she might have been, and was deliberately ignored at the fateful Munich Conference. Not until April 1939 did Britain and France reluctantly begin negotiations for a Russian alliance. Even then they were not prepared to accept the Russian demand to send troops into Poland, Finland, and the small Baltic states, the outposts against German attack which Russia had lost after World War I. The Munich Agreement in September 1938, when Britain and France tried to conciliate Hitler by recognising his demands for a large portion of Czech territory, seemed to Stalin to be an attempt to direct German expansion eastwards against Russia and away from the West. He was fully aware that Hitler's eventual purpose was the seizure of all Russian territory in Europe, but the Red Army in 1939, after recent purges, was unprepared for large-scale conflict. A long and exhausting war between Russia's capitalist enemies, Germany, Poland, Britain, and France, promised, moreover, time, security, and profit for the Soviet Union. The result was the Soviet-German non-aggression pact of August 1939. In return for Russian neutrality Hitler acknowledged Russia's right to seize Finland, Estonia, Latvia, Lithuania, and eastern Poland, areas which he gambled on recovering by the later defeat of Russia (see Map 2). By this action Stalin ensured the outbreak of World War II and the crushing of Poland, a factor which the Western powers found difficult to forgive or forget.

In the early months of the war supplies of grain and oil flowed from Russia to her German ally, and the Soviet Union was expelled from the League of Nations for its attack upon Finland in November 1939. Until Hitler's invasion of Russia in June 1941, the struggle against Germany and Italy was denounced by Russian propaganda as an 'imperialist war'. Only in the face of a common enemy were Britain, Russia, and America thrown together in the military alliances of 1941 and 1942. Churchill's spontaneous offer of support to Russia in June 1941, the British Arctic convoys, and massive American Lease-Lend aid helped temporarily to submerge Russia's deep-rooted suspicions, while the heroism of the Red Army and the epic battle of Stalingrad won Western admiration and respect. Beneath the surface, however, the divisions and tensions remained.

Although Russia received much material help from her new partners she obtained little direct military assistance. Russian demands for a Second Front in Europe to relieve German pressure upon her remained unanswered until the 'D-Day' landings of June

4   Soldiers of the Red Army in Austria meet Russian girls whom they have freed from Nazi captivity

1944. When the Western powers decided in 1942 to delay the Second Front and launch a major campaign in North Africa and Italy it appeared to Stalin that his allies were more anxious to forestall Russian influence in south-eastern Europe while Russia bled to death in the bitter struggle with Germany. There was much truth in Western claims that they were not strong enough to invade Western Europe and that Italy was weak, but grave suspicions remained.

Both sides, too, remembering the diplomatic negotiations of 1939, feared that the other would try to make a separate peace with Germany. This feeling was evident when the leaders of the Grand Alliance met in February 1945 at the Crimean health resort of Yalta to plan the final attack on Germany and discuss the problems of a provisional peace settlement. Serious differences emerged over the future of Poland. Britain and France had declared war in September 1939 to protect Polish independence. Even with the Germans invading in 1941, Stalin had demanded British recognition of his right to eastern Poland, lost after a Polish attack on Russia in 1920, and briefly regained in 1939. He had, however, eventually reached an agreement with the exiled Polish government in London, but as the Russians advanced into Poland in early 1944 they set up at Lublin a rival Communist government. In Warsaw in September 1944 the Polish Home Army, loyal to the London government, decided to drive out the Germans first and resist the Russians afterwards. The advancing Red Army held back until the Germans had crushed the rising and destroyed the only Polish force loyal to the London government before it occupied the city.

At Yalta Stalin revived his demand for the Polish eastern provinces, and insisted that Poland should be compensated by German territory east of the Oder and Neisse rivers, the port of Danzig, and the southern part of East Prussia (see Map 2). He also stipulated that any new Polish government must be 'friendly' to Russia.

'Twice in the last thirty years', he stated, 'our enemies the Germans have passed through this corridor. It is in Russia's interests that Poland should be strong and powerful, in a position to shut the door . . . by her own force.'

In many respects Russia's demands were not unreasonable. The European war had reached a critical stage. Japan was, as yet, undefeated. Churchill and the American President Roosevelt were still uncertain of progress in making the atomic bomb. Russian aid seemed crucial for speedy victory in the East. Memories of the German-Soviet pact survived, and Russia's great successes in Europe created fears of a separate peace with Germany as had happened in 1918. Polish independence was forgotten; broad agreement was given to the Russian demands, and the Grand Alliance survived for a few further months. An even worse rift threatened a few weeks later when Stalin learned that Field Marshal Alexander was to meet the German Field Marshal Kesselring at Berne to discuss German surrender in Italy. The Russians were convinced that their Western allies intended to make a separate peace which would allow German troops to move to the Russian front, and a breach was only narrowly avoided.

During the last 18 months of the European war as the Russians advanced on the Eastern front, Winston Churchill, a longstanding opponent of the Soviet régime, grew increasingly alarmed about Russian policy. The circumstances of war threatened to advance Russia's traditional imperial ambitions in Eastern Europe, the Balkans, and the Black Sea area, including Turkey and the Persian Gulf, with their control of Middle Eastern oil. He vainly tried to persuade the Americans that Western military strength should be used to defeat the Nazis and simultaneously curb the expansion of Russian power. Only in Greece, where British troops occupied Athens and crushed a rising by

the Communist resistance movement in October 1944, was his policy successful. This action drew strong criticism from America. For the Americans, contemptuous of secret diplomacy, and newcomers to the European political scene, the main consideration was to bring the war to a speedy end enabling America to return to 'normalcy' and isolation. America had no political objectives in Europe and believed military commanders should not be hindered by political matters. President Roosevelt, an unselfish idealist, had none of Churchill's suspicions. He was convinced he could handle the Russians, who he thought had no aggressive ambitions, and by the establishment of a United Nations Organisation preserve world peace. America and Russia appeared to have much in common. Both were republics and both disliked colonialism.

Churchill's plan to launch the Second Front through the Balkans, the apparent area of Russia's ambitions, which could have prevented the Cold War, fell on deaf ears. The postponement of 'D-Day' until June 1944, when the Russian advance into Eastern Europe was forging ahead, meant that the invasion of Germany became a race between Russia and the Western powers to reach Berlin and the Balkans first. Once over the Rhine Churchill was anxious to meet the Russians 'as far east as possible', and to reach Berlin and Prague together with, if not before, them. The Americans, however, were not prepared to compete. Prague could have been reached first and American forces were at the Elbe, 53 miles from Berlin, before the Russians had crossed the Oder, but in each case they held back (see Map 1). When the fighting ceased the Russians had added 24 million people to the Soviet Union by the recapture of the Baltic states, eastern Poland, Bessarabia, Bukhovina, and parts of Finland and East Prussia. Russian armies were also in Poland, Czechoslovakia, Bulgaria, Yugoslavia, Hungary, Romania, Albania, and Austria in addition to the eastern portion of Germany (see Map 2). In many of these East European lands, containing 100 million people, there were disturbing signs that the military occupation would be used to support local Communists in national government as had already happened in Poland. This conflicted strongly with the Atlantic Charter of 1941 to which Britain, Russia, and America had subscribed stating that they sought no territorial gain and supported the right of all peoples to choose their own form of government.

To Churchill in May 1945 the only alternative was for Britain and America to use their combined military power to resist the Soviet Union. Although they had held back, the armies of the Western powers were still well to the east of the line across Germany

Legend

- (shaded) Territory seized by Russia 1945
- (hatched) States which had become Communist by 1949
- (thick line) The Iron Curtain

300 miles
500 km

NORWAY

FINLAND

KARELIA

Leningrad

SWEDEN

ESTONIA

LATVIA

To Russia 1945

LITHUANIA

GREAT BRITAIN

NETHERLANDS

DENMARK

Bremen

Danzig

EAST PRUSSIA

Minsk

BELGIUM

R. Rhine

Stettin

Berlin

To Poland 1945

Warsaw

U. S. S. R.

BRITISH ZONE

RUSSIAN ZONE

Bonn

EUPEN & MALMEDY

GERMANY

Odor-Neisse Line

POLAND

Lublin

EASTERN POLAND

To Russia 1945

FRENCH ZONE

AMERICAN ZONE

Nuremberg

SUDETENLAND

Prague

CZECHOSLOVAKIA

ALSACE LORRAINE

FRANCE

SWITZERLAND

U.S. ZONE

RUSSIAN ZONE

Vienna

FRENCH ZONE

AUSTRIA

BRITISH ZONE

HUNGARY

Budapest

BUKHOVINA

BESSARABIA

Marseilles

YUGOSLAVIA

Belgrade

ROMANIA

Bucharest

BLACK SEA

ITALY

ADRIATIC SEA

R. Danube

Bosphorus

ALBANIA

BULGARIA

Sofia

MEDITERRANEAN SEA

Salonika

GREECE

Dardanelles

TURKEY

Athens

MAP NO. 2   DIVIDED EUROPE

14

which it had been agreed that the Russians should reach. Churchill wished to delay withdrawal until a democratic settlement was reached in Eastern Europe. As Germany crumbled British and American troops were being rapidly moved east to fight the Japanese. Demobilisation was also beginning. At Yalta Roosevelt had announced that he would not keep troops in Germany over two years. By 1947 it seemed inevitable that Russian forces in Germany, only a few hundred miles from the Rhine, would greatly outnumber those of the West and be in a position to sweep across Europe to the Channel coast. If Russian domination of Europe was to be avoided now was the time to make a stand. On 12 April Roosevelt had died suddenly on the eve of victory. Five days after the German surrender, as the Russians grew more truculent, Churchill despatched his famous 'Iron Curtain' telegram to Harry S. Truman, Roosevelt's successor:

> I am profoundly concerned about the European situation. . . . An iron curtain is drawn down upon their front. We do not know what is going on behind. . . . Surely it is vital now to come to an understanding with Russia . . . before we weaken our armies . . . or retire to the zones of occupation . . . this issue . . . seems to me to dwarf all others. . . .[1]

The time was not right and the telegram received no favourable response. It is doubtful if either British or American public opinion would have accepted such a policy in the hour of jubilation. The Japanese war was not over. Truman, a little-known Missouri farmer and businessman, had no experience of foreign affairs and could, for the time being, only continue the assumptions and policies of his predecessor. He, perhaps rightly, assumed that Britain was too concerned with her own position in the post-war world. American Lease-Lend aid to Russia abruptly ceased, but American and British forces withdrew westwards in some cases as much as 150 miles.

Churchill could only acquiesce. Britain had ruined herself in two costly world wars. Many of her overseas investments which had been used to buy food and raw materials were gone. Her navy was no longer mistress of the seas, and her empire was bound for early break-up. In military strength she was much inferior to America upon whom she relied heavily for post-war economic aid. France and her empire were similarly placed. The destiny of the world had passed into the hands of the two 'super-powers', much greater in size, population, and natural resources, that had emerged from World War II.

History and geography had made the 'super-powers' completely different. America, in her short history, had always been strong and safe, making her people self-confident and free to develop a system of democracy. A pioneering tradition had given Americans a strong belief in free business enterprise. Rapid industrialisation and an abundant land had made the U.S.A. the richest capitalist country in the world. By 1945 she controlled a third of the world's industrial production and half the world's shipping.

Russia's history and geography on the other hand had given her a centralised, authoritarian system of government, and a deep fear of the outside world. Without defensible western frontiers Russia had suffered ten centuries of devastation by invaders. Magyars, Bulgars, Tartars, Lithuanians, Poles, Swedes, Napoleon's French, and the Kaiser's Germans had in turn wrought their havoc before Russia became the world's first Communist state in 1917. After the revolution came the Western capitalist 'intervention' of British, Americans, Japanese, French, and Poles, and finally Hitler's onslaught of 1941. Before 1917 Russia had survived by placing power in the hands of one man, a Tsar, and by trying to expand her frontiers westwards to secure adequate defence. After the revolution, the Tsar was replaced by a Communist dictator, and expansion was

[1] Winston S. Churchill, *The Second World War*, Vol VI: *Triumph and Tragedy* (Cassell), pp. 498–9.

6 In spring 1945 Russian tanks ring
Berlin before their final thrust of the war

7 The Russian army was intent on
advancing as far west as possible and
holding on to territorial gains

further encouraged by the threat of Western capitalist destruction and the mission of
spreading world communism. The development of a protective barrier of states against
the West had begun with the invasion of Poland and Finland in 1939. World War II,
regarded by Russia as a truce with Western capitalism, gave her the chance of expanding
westwards to an extent which would make her permanently safe, particularly from a
revived Germany, which she feared the most. In Western eyes, however, Russia came
to seem intent upon world domination for communism, although this was probably
secondary to her own security.

With the defeat of Germany, Russians came again to feel that the capitalist threat
was very real. This feeling increased with the dramatic revelation of capitalism's new
weapon, the atomic bomb, whose existence had been kept from Russia, and whose
secrets of manufacture the United States announced she intended to preserve as a
'sacred trust'. The American occupation of Japan and the growth of American Pacific
bases increased the Russian fear of encirclement. A massive effort began to catch up in
the development of atomic weapons.

> Even now after the greatest victory known to history [announced President
> Kalinin] we cannot for one moment forget . . . that our country remains the one
> socialist state in the world. . . . Only the . . . most immediate danger which threatened
> us from . . . Germany has disappeared. . . . .[1]

At the last war-time meeting of the 'Big Three' at Potsdam in August 1945 major
differences still remained submerged. Japan's defeat and the atomic bomb had yet to
come. Midway through the conference, Churchill, defeated in a British general election,
was replaced by the Labour leader, Clement Attlee, who like President Truman was
new to the highest office. America also did not yet see clearly the role she had to play in
the tense, world-wide power contest which was to come. As in 1918, the overwhelming
American desire was to return to 'normalcy', which meant rapid demobilisation, withdrawal from Europe, and a quick return to pre-war international trade and foreign
relations. This in turn meant the speedy signing of peace treaties with Germany and her
allies.

[1] Quoted ed. J. L. Henderson, *Since 1945* (Methuen), p. 76.

8 Autumn 1944. Polish soldiers help the Russians to clear the last Germans out of a Warsaw suburb. Poland was to fall entirely within Moscow's orbit

To most Americans the main hope for 'winning the peace' lay still with the United Nations Organisation. Roosevelt had hoped that in the post-war world freedom of expression and worship; freedom from want and from fear, would be enforced by the co-operation of the world's 'Four Policemen' – America, Russia, Britain, and China – within a United Nations Organisation. The term 'United Nations' had first been used in January 1942 when 26 Allied nations had supported these principles. 21 months later representatives of the 'Four Policemen' had recognised the need for 'establishing . . . a general international organisation . . . for the maintenance of international peace and security'. At a further conference at Dumbarton Oaks, U.S.A., in November 1944 the four Great Powers designed the new organisation and agreed that their proposals should be put in a Charter. The new organisation was named the United Nations and its Charter was signed by 50 nations at the San Francisco Conference of April–June 1945. By their signatures they promised 'to save succeeding generations from the scourge of war', and recognised certain basic human rights and 'the equal rights of . . . nations large and small'.

To preserve international peace and security and get international co-operation over economic, social, cultural, and human problems the United Nations had a General Assembly, a Security Council, an Economic and Social Council, a Trusteeship Council, an International Court of Justice, and a Secretariat. These bodies were in many ways similar to those of the old League of Nations which they replaced. The General Assembly, where all member states had equal voting power, was to discuss and make recommendations to the Security Council on all matters concerning world peace. The Security Council consisted of America, Russia, Britain, China, and France plus six non-permanent members from other states elected in rotation for two years by the General Assembly. Functioning continuously, its task was to deal with any dispute likely to endanger world security. It could call upon members to take joint armed action against any aggressor. All five permanent members, however, had to agree for any major issue to pass the Council. The right of 'veto' over major issues was thought necessary by Russia, who in the first General Assembly formed with her supporters a small minority. Former enemy and neutral powers were excluded, while the nations of

9 June 1945. President
Truman addresses
the last session of the
U.N. Conference
on International
Organisation

Africa and Asia were not yet independent. The U.S.A. on the other hand commanded the votes of the 21 Latin American republics, China, and the Philippines, and Britain was supported by the Commonwealth nations.

The success of the U.N. depended upon the co-operation of the 'Policemen' who had worked successfully together in war. There was little of the widespread optimism at San Francisco which had marked the formation of the League of Nations in 1919. Nevertheless, the prospects seemed more promising since both America and Russia, notable absentees in 1919, had given their support from the beginning.

These hopes were soon dashed. Even before the General Assembly held its first meeting in January 1946, the Council of Foreign Ministers, set up at Potsdam to prepare draft peace treaties for Germany's European allies, had broken up in deadlock on 2 October 1945. Russia's demand for trusteeship of the former Italian territory of Tripolitania, which would have given her a 'warm-water' port in the Mediterranean, was refused by Britain, while America would not sign treaties with Bulgaria and Romania as she objected to their Russian-sponsored governments.

> For over four years [explained John Foster Dulles to puzzled Americans] every meeting of . . . the great powers . . . gave the impression that complete harmony had been achieved. That was a war diet of soothing syrup. . . . There have always been differences which are now coming to light.[1]

The Grand Alliance was over, and when Americans had accepted the idea of a divided world a Cold War would begin in which two armed camps constantly matched strength with each other throughout the world. The Cold War would be fought with economic and propaganda weapons; with diplomacy and limited war. Always, however, the contestants would draw back from a final conflict for in the Atomic Age if the war became 'hot' it could result only in mutual destruction.

[1] Keesing's Contemporary Archives, p. 7474.

2 Towards Cold War

IT TOOK TIME, however, for American public opinion, conditioned by war-time propaganda, to accept the end of 'Great Power unity'. Privately many American statesmen already had grave doubts about Russia's post-war intentions, but they did not express them too forcibly in public. Demobilisation continued apace. By June 1946 America's armed forces had been reduced from 12 million to 3 million men. A year later they stood at $1\frac{1}{2}$ million. While the armies of democracy melted away there was no corresponding reduction in Russian strength.

It was therefore against Britain that Russian hostility was mainly directed in the months that followed the end of the war. In the Middle East, traditionally a British sphere of influence, Russia demanded the revision of the Montreux Convention which in 1936 had placed control of the Dardanelles and Bosphorus in Turkish hands. Russian troops remaining in northern Iran after the American withdrawal tried to sponsor a breakaway movement which would bring the area under Soviet control. In the Security Council Russia denounced the presence of British troops in Greece, which were preventing a takeover by the Communist resistance movement from the British puppet government. Strong demands came also for the withdrawal of French and British troops from Syria and the Lebanon. As Russian pressure mounted in the Middle East, British ships were mined in the Corfu Channel off the coast of Communist Albania.

Nevertheless, Americans began to grow perceptibly more disturbed at the aggressive Russian actions which belied Roosevelt's optimism for the post-war world and seemed contrary to the idea of 'Socialism in one country'. At Yalta, the Western powers had had no choice but to accept Russian influence in the East European countries which her armies had occupied prior to the conclusion of formal peace treaties. In the same way they had established for themselves similar rights in Italy and Greece. In all these countries the 'Big Three' had agreed to the formation of provisional coalition governments, which would have the maximum support necessary to solve the immediate post-war problems before the holding of free democratic elections. Such 'Popular Front' governments appeared in both Eastern and Western Europe. In the former, however, it soon became obvious that genuine coalitions were being deliberately subverted in a 'cold' Communist revolution, often actively assisted by the presence of the Red Army.

In Yugoslavia and Albania subversion was unnecessary since the Communists were already in power before the war ended. In Yugoslavia Marshal Tito had led his Communist partisans to victory against both the Axis powers and General Mihailovic, the nationalist 'Chetnik' leader and representative of the old régime. His power was based upon unquestioned support from the peasantry, strong national sentiment, and traditional Serbian sympathy for Russia. His National Liberation Front, established in March 1945, at first included a number of non-Communists, but these soon disappeared. The Communist Party, whose members held the key positions of state, became the only political party allowed. The monarchy was abolished and a republic proclaimed in November 1945. A new constitution based upon that of the Soviet Union was adopted the following January. Mihailovic, the monarchist who in his attempts to defeat the Communists was said to have collaborated with the Axis, was captured and shot in July 1946. A series of political trials followed in which prominent leaders of

Yugoslavia's pre-war parties were charged with treason on behalf of the Western powers and all opposition was removed to Tito's one-party state.

In feudal, tribal Albania, which in 1939 had changed little since the Middle Ages, communism also emerged triumphant in 1945. The mountaineers of the National Liberation Front formed by Communist schoolmaster Enver Hoxha in 1942, and modelled upon Tito's partisans, defeated a rival nationalist resistance movement which, like the Chetniks, had given its support to the Germans. As the Germans left Hoxha took control and in January 1946 Albania became a Communist republic. Relations with the West rapidly deteriorated, partly because of the Western refusal to surrender exiled nationalist leaders and partly because the Greek government, which was supported by British troops, laid claim to southern Albania. The American legation left Albania in November 1946, and relations with Britain ended in early 1947.

In the remaining Eastern European countries the Communists also gradually gained the ascendancy. This resulted partly from circumstances and partly from calculated planning. In most countries there was a natural reaction against Nazism and a desire for land reform which temporarily won support for communism, particularly as many landowners and industrialists had collaborated with the Germans.

Almost everywhere Communist strategy followed a similar pattern. Initially the Communists took part in a genuine coalition of several democratic parties. These coalition governments were pledged to remove from public life all pro-Nazi and anti-Soviet elements, and also to secure Russian lines of communication with eastern Germany. The old ruling classes of Eastern Europe, whose record of collaboration left them no defence, were thus destroyed. During this first stage the Communists also secured control of the army, police, and propaganda departments which enabled them to begin the second stage of their seizure of power. This involved the formation of bogus coalition governments in which non-Communists still participated but which in practice were chosen by the Communist Party. The peasant parties, standing for small, private ownership, and the middle-class liberal parties, both of which had considerable support, were driven into opposition. This was still permitted but became increasingly difficult with press censorship and the disruption of political meetings which was ignored by the police. In the background, ready if necessary, was the Red Army.

Genuine coalitions lasted only briefly in Romania and Bulgaria. In the former

10 Enver Hoxha of Albania, surrounded   11 Josip Broz Tito of Yugoslavia
by children at a Party function

the Communists pressed the coalition leader, General Radescu, immediately to begin land reform. When he refused, a political crisis developed in February 1945. The Communists attacked him as a Fascist, and he in turn denounced them at public meetings. There were armed clashes in Bucharest between supporters of the National Peasant Party and Communist workers. The Russians, fearing treachery in the Romanian army, disarmed Romanian forces in the capital. Romania was the corridor to Hungary, where at this time the Red Army was faring badly. Andrei Vyshinsky, the Russian deputy Foreign Minister, demanded that the King should dismiss Radescu. He yielded on 6 March and the Radescu coalition was replaced by a National Democratic Front under the Communist Groza. When Britain and America refused to recognise this government, which was contrary to the Yalta agreement, two non-Communists were appointed to the government in January 1946. These newcomers were, however, completely ignored, and a campaign of terror began against the National Peasant and Liberal parties.

In Bulgaria the Fatherland Front coalition, which had seized control during the revolution of September 1944, first eliminated the leaders of the Fascist régime. Among the 5,500 who were executed or imprisoned the Communist Minister of the Interior also included a number of prominent democrats. Opposition to the Communists was centred around the peasant Agrarian Union led by Nikola Petkov and the Social Democrats (socialists). By August 1945 both parties had been subverted by the Communists and their leaders driven from the coalition. Stage one was over and in September 1946 the unpopular monarchy was replaced by a republic. When elections for the National Assembly were held in October many leading non-Communists were already in jail. Not surprisingly the Fatherland Front secured a notable victory and the Communist leader, Georgi Dimitrov, hero of the Reichstag Fire Trial in 1933, became Prime Minister. His first action was to begin the final liquidation of the opposition.

The genuine Hungarian coalition survived somewhat longer. In the wake of the Soviet armies had come a number of Hungarian Communists, including several survivors from the short-lived Hungarian Communist régime of 1919. These soon made contact with Communist organisers of the resistance and joined a coalition with the Social Democrats, Smallholders' Party, and the National Peasant Party. In this coalition the Communists secured control of the police and the Ministry of Agriculture, where Imre Nagy immediately began the long-overdue process of land reform. The trade unions, too, soon passed under Communist control. Their new leader, Stephen Kossov, was a Budapest tramworker who had been captured by the Russians and received his political training in Moscow. Opposition to the Communists came, as elsewhere, from the peasants of the Smallholders' Party who secured a sizeable majority in a parliamentary election in the autumn of 1945. The coalition, however, continued. Zoltan Tildy, leader of the Smallholders, became President of the new Hungarian republic and Ferenc Nagy, another Smallholders' leader, was made Prime Minister.

The Communist leader, Matyas Rakosi, insisted, however, that Imre Nagy should become Minister of the Interior and gradually Communist control of the police increased. In March 1946 the Smallholders' Party was purged by the Russian authorities who claimed it contained Fascists. On 26 February 1947 Bela Kovacs, secretary of the Smallholders, was arrested by Soviet soldiers on a charge of espionage. British and American protests were ignored. Ferenc Nagy, supposedly incriminated by his friend Kovacs, was also forced to resign. The coalition was over, and both the Smallholders' and National Peasant parties were broken.

In Poland, although the Provisional Government of National Unity set up with a Communist majority in June 1945 included Stanislaus Mikolajczyk and other Peasant Party leaders, there was only a pretence at coalition. The nationalist Polish Peasant Party was stronger than peasant parties elsewhere. In the tense days at the close of the war Russia feared that if conflict came with the West the latter would be aided by nationalist Poles. The remnants of the Polish Home Army were, therefore, ruthlessly hunted down. Communist control of all key government departments had been assured by the Lublin Committee. The Peasant Party was widely persecuted and despite British and American protests a provisional constitution on Soviet lines was adopted in February 1947.

The only exceptions in this pattern of Communist East European revolution were Czechoslovakia and Finland. In Czechoslovakia the Communists formed a People's Front coalition with the Social Democrats, National Socialists, and People's Catholic Party. The Agrarian Party, which before 1938 had received much peasant and business support, was dissolved since it had collaborated with Germany after Munich. From the outset the Communists controlled the army and the Ministries of the Interior, Agriculture, and Education. A takeover would have been possible in 1945 but the Communist leader, Klement Gottwald, held back. Feeling against the West was still strong from the Munich desertion. The expulsion of the Bohemian Germans and the redistribution of their land and property won much support among the peasantry and working classes. The Russians left in December 1945 and Gottwald's confidence seemed justified when the Communists secured a large majority in the parliamentary elections of May 1946. Gottwald, a former carpenter and Czech Communist leader since 1929, became Prime Minister, but the coalition continued.

Finnish Communists secured about a quarter of the seats in the Finnish parliament in March 1945, and for the next three years took part in a coalition with Social Democrats and peasant representatives. Even when the Communists were swept from ministerial office in July 1948, however, there was no Soviet intervention. The Finns, for whose stubbornness the Russians had a healthy respect, bowed unlike the nationalist Poles to the harsh realities of power. President Paasikivi made no demands which would

12   Klement Gottwald
announces that the
Czechoslovak
Communists have taken
over the government
(*see page 32*).
His brutal methods are
not forgotten in
Czechoslovakia

upset his powerful neighbour. Stalin's fears about Baltic security were allayed. Russian domination seemed unnecessary and Finland survived as a self-governing democracy.

Soviet activities in Eastern Europe were matched in the Pacific by the American denial to the Russians of any share in the control of post-war Japan. The Western powers, still uncertain at Yalta whether Japan could be defeated without Russian aid, had made concessions which they might not otherwise have given. Russia had deliberately delayed her entry into the Pacific war until she had been forced into action by the dropping of the A-bomb and the fear that she would be excluded from the Far Eastern settlement. For a six-day campaign in which her losses were slight she regained the Kurile Islands and Sakhalin which she had lost to Japan in 1905 (see Map 4). The Western powers, who had profited to some extent by Russia's enormous material and human losses in the European fighting, were left feeling they had paid a high price for unnecessary support. Although in theory Japan was jointly occupied by the Allies, in practice American forces under General MacArthur remained, despite Russian protests, in sole control. Japanese politics and industry were reorganised along American lines, a process which aroused similar Russian fears to those of the West over the creation of a bloc of Russian 'satellites' in Eastern Europe.

If American statesmen were quick to see Japan as a potential buffer against Russian expansion they failed to see completely the effects of the war in Europe. Here the Allied policy of 'unconditional surrender' laid down at the Casablanca Conference in 1943, had not only destroyed Germany, but also the European balance of power, and had left in Germany a power vacuum in which East and West were to come face to face. In the past Russia's power in Europe had been balanced by either one or a combination of continental mainland powers. In the twentieth century Germany had played this part. Now Germany had gone. Britain and France were too weak to fill the vacuum, and European stability which had been endangered by Napoleon, the Kaiser, and Hitler was again threatened by the dominance of one power for the fourth time in 150 years.

There was no general peace conference after World War II as there had been in 1919. At the Potsdam Conference arrangements for a settlement were left largely in the hands of the Council of Foreign Ministers dominated by America, Russia, and Britain. After bitter wrangling, peace treaties were produced for Italy, Finland, Hungary, Romania, and Bulgaria which were signed in February 1947. Each treaty stipulated the payment of heavy reparations principally to Russia. These she used to prolong the economic dependence of Finland and the Eastern European states. Russia also gained northern Bukhovina and Bessarabia from Romania, and Karelia and the naval base of Petsamo from Finland (see Map 2). A decision to make the Danube and Black Sea open waterways, however, aroused bitter Russian resistance. The Danube was the main trade route between the Balkans and the West. Control over it would have meant full Russian control of Balkan economic life. Unrestricted foreign entry to the Black Sea laid the Crimea and the ports of southern Russia open to attack as had been seen in the Crimean War a century before. Western insistence upon this matter was inevitably interpreted as sinister.

A peace treaty with Austria should not have proved difficult. The Great Powers had agreed in 1943 that since Austria had been forcibly absorbed into Germany in 1938 she should be re-established as a 'free and independent state'. The Russian armies in April 1945 had set up a provisional government for the Austrian republic which after elections became a successful coalition of Catholics and socialists. Russian dealings with

13 Vienna, 1945. American and Russian members of the occupying forces stand by a Stalin hoarding in front of the Opera House

the three Western powers on the joint Allied Council were perfectly amicable but she refused all attempts to end the four-power occupation of Austria by a peace treaty. Austria was of strategic importance since it covered the southern Czech frontier and was thus a part of the Russian system of security. It was also a rich source for the extraction of crude oil and machinery in the form of reparations which would help to repair the shattered Russian economy. Austria, like Germany, therefore remained divided.

The problem of a German peace treaty was the most difficult question of all. At Potsdam the 'Big Three' had provisionally agreed upon the division of Germany prior to a final peace treaty. Germany's eastern boundary had been tentatively re-drawn along the line of the Oder–Neisse rivers. Russia was to take the northern part of East Prussia while Danzig and the other German territory east of the Oder–Neisse line passed to Poland. The Sudetenland was restored to Czechoslovakia, Alsace-Lorraine to France, and Eupen and Malmédy to Belgium (see Map 2). For occupation purposes Germany was divided into four zones corresponding roughly to the areas in which the Great Powers had fought. Administrative authority was vested in the four commanders-in-chief who made up the Allied Control Council meeting in Berlin to discuss common problems and interests. Berlin itself, lying deep in the Russian zone, was similarly divided under the control of a four-power 'Kommandatura'. Theoretically the function of the Allied Control Council was to maintain German unity, to disarm and de-militarise Germany, and to prepare the way for German reconstruction on a demo-cratic basis. At first hopes ran high. 'Berlin, we were convinced,' stated Eisenhower, 'was an experimental laboratory for the development of international accord'.[1]

Russian and Western policies were, however, incompatible. The occupying

[1] General D. Eisenhower, *Crusade in Europe* (Heinemann), p. 500.

powers were left free to satisfy their reparations demands from their own zones. Russia from the outset was determined for security reasons to keep Germany weak, and also to extract the maximum compensation for German war-damage in Russia. In March 1946 the Great Powers agreed upon the amount of industrialisation to be allowed in Germany. The remaining plant and machinery were to serve as reparations and were allocated principally to Russia. The majority of the machinery had to come from the British and American zones. In return the British and Americans expected food for their zones from the agricultural Russian zone. None, however, was forthcoming, and the Russians proceeded not only to take machinery from the Western zones but also to strip their own East German zone of what plant it contained without informing the Control Council. The cost of food supplies for the Western zones had to be met by America and Britain. This the latter, on the verge of economic breakdown, could not afford. On 3 May 1946 General Clay, Eisenhower's deputy on the Control Council, refused to allow further Russian reparations in machinery from the Western zones.

This serious breach between the victors was accompanied by a political division of Germany. In its Eastern zone, Russia began the forcible imposition of German communism. The first stage in this process was the fusion of German Communists and Social Democrats into the Socialist Unity Party (S.E.D.) in April 1946. This was accomplished by pressure upon the socialist leaders. The chief of these, Otto Grotewohl, a former printer imprisoned by the Nazis in 1933, gave way. The new party, led by Grotewohl and Walter Ulbricht, a Communist who had spent the years of Nazi rule in Moscow, was under complete Communist control. The land of Prussian landlords was confiscated and many large industries were nationalised. Attempts by the S.E.D. to extend its control to the Western zones of Berlin by a merger with the Social Democrats there forced the Americans and British to stir themselves to protect West German democracy. Communist control of Berlin would have been followed by the extension of

14   On his return from Germany in 1949 General Lucius Clay was decorated by President Truman at a ceremony in the White House

25

Communist power throughout the whole of the Western zones. This the democratic German political parties such as Konrad Adenauer's Christian Democratic Union and Karl Schumacher's Social Democratic Party were already pledged to resist. The West Berlin Social Democrats themselves refused the merger, and the Communists thus lost all chance of an electoral victory in Berlin. At the Berlin municipal elections of October 1946 they were heavily defeated by the Social Democrats. Berliners thus rejected the absorption of their city, already isolated from West Germany, into the Soviet zone, and Communist hopes of uniting Germany under a Communist-dominated government were destroyed. When attempts were made to intimidate the Berlin Council whose meeting place lay in the Russian zone, its seat of government was moved to West Berlin while a rival Communist administration was established in East Berlin.

Britain and America had hoped to bring about German recovery by pooling the resources of the different zones before finally giving the Germans political responsibility on a democratic basis. It was also clear that Germany's economic revival was vital for the economic recovery of Western Europe. Russia on the other hand was intent upon keeping Germany weak.

Gradually as their divisions deepened the Great Powers' fear of Germany was replaced by their fears of each other. Both sides began to try to win the Germans as allies, and inevitably they began to organise their zones in their own image thus emphasising the difference between them. In the West, America, Britain, and France began the process of building a new democratic Germany. In the East, communisation rapidly increased. No peace treaty was signed. Instead as the Grand Alliance broke down the political and economic division of Germany became deeper, and by 1947 the vanquished nation had become a central battleground in the Cold War between East and West.

15   Otto Grotewohl, the East German Prime Minister, at a banquet on a visit to China. *On the left*, Mao Tse-Tung; *on the right*, Chou En-Lai

3 Crisis and Containment 1947

AT THE CLOSE OF 1946, despite the growing differences over Germany, the presence of American troops in both Austria and Germany was still regarded as temporary. America had undertaken no obligation to support any state in Europe or Asia in its resistance to communism. British troops in Egypt, Palestine, and Greece were, it was supposed, capable of protecting British interests in the Middle East.

The weakness of Britain and the post-war advance of communism in Western Europe seemingly passed unnoticed. At the French general elections in November 1946 the Communist Party had emerged as the largest single party in France with 168 seats in the National Assembly. Outstanding work in the resistance movement, unemployment, and the need for social reform had swollen its membership by over a million. By January 1947 not only was it playing a leading part in a Popular Front government, but the vice-premier and Minister of Defence were Communists. In Italy and Belgium powerful Communist parties also shared power in coalition Popular Front governments.

The British economy, after five years of war, was on the brink of collapse. Bread and flour had been rationed in mid-1946 to enable supplies to be sent to Germany while the worst summer rains for 20 years had seriously damaged the British harvest. In November 1946 Britain had thought it necessary to add to her burden the introduction of conscription. British troops had been in Greece since October 1944. As the Germans had evacuated, the Communist-dominated National Liberation Front had taken control. The Communists were persuaded with difficulty to join the exiled politicians recognised by the British in a government of National Unity. When attempts were made to disarm them in favour of a new right-wing army the Communist forces attempted to seize Athens in December 1944. After two months heavy fighting they were

16   General George Marshall, U.S. Secretary of State, whose programme of economic aid saved Western Europe from collapse after World War II

driven out by British troops and forced to accept disarmament. The British suffered over 1,000 casualties, but large areas of Greece still remained under Communist control.

The truce was temporary. The election of a right-wing government in March 1946, which began a persecution of left-wing sympathisers, was the signal for a renewal of the civil war. The Communists withdrew to the northern mountains where they were provided with arms and supplies by Albania, Yugoslavia, and Bulgaria. Government control was soon reduced to Salonika and the area around Athens. As thousands of refugees flooded into these districts it became obvious that without constant British military and economic aid the Greek government would collapse.

17 Greek government forces firing 25-pounders in action against the Communists near the Bulgarian frontier

18 Greek government commandos pass peasant women in the mountains of central Greece

Stalin had shown little interest in the activities of the Greek Communists during the war. He was equally disinterested in their attempted takeover in post-war Greece. Not only were General Markos and his Communist guerrillas beyond Moscow's control but they threatened to antagonise Britain and America while Stalin was heavily preoccupied with the situation in Germany and Eastern Europe. They therefore received no Russian support. To harassed contemporaries, however, the civil war in Greece appeared a serious threat to Italy and the Mediterranean, and yet another stage in the advance towards Russian world domination. This fear was strengthened by the Soviet attitude towards Turkey (see Map 2).

In the summer of 1945 Russia had demanded the return of Kars and Ardahan in eastern Anatolia, which had been Russian territories from 1878 to 1918, together with naval bases in the Bosphorus and Dardanelles. If Greece fell to communism Turkey would be surrounded. Soviet pressure upon Turkey mounted throughout 1946 and there were threats of force. If this came Turkey could not resist. Russia therefore seemed intent upon dominating the Middle East with its rich oil deposits and central strategic position between Europe, Asia, and Africa.

The crisis culminated in the terrible winter of 1946–7 which brought complete dislocation to Britain and the countries of Western Europe. A fuel crisis had already

28

been developing in Britain in the closing weeks of 1946. Shortage of manpower in the pits; low coal stocks; and the increased demand for fuel and power created by the end of the war were all factors which were intensified by the severest winter weather for a hundred years. From the second week in January 1947 severe snowstorms swept the country, leaving roads and railways blocked, towns and villages isolated, and coal stocks at the lowest level ever recorded. By the first week in February temperatures had fallen below freezing point and the whole country was paralysed and icebound. Cuts in domestic and industrial supplies of electricity saw the 'Blackout' return as street lighting was extinguished. The B.B.C. ceased broadcasting and everywhere factories closed or

19   A car stuck in snow-drifts in southern England during the terrible winter of early 1947

were reduced indefinitely to short-time working. 2 million workers were sent home. Troops attempting to transport coal from the pitheads were hampered by thick fog. Power supplies to industry were not resumed until 3 March by which time the weather had reduced Britain and Western Europe to the point of economic and social breakdown. Britain's financial situation left her incapable of further aid to Greece or Turkey, and on 28 February 1947, her government informed America that this aid would cease by the end of the following month. Britain, which had borne the brunt of two world wars, was 'like a wounded soldier bleeding to death', while a Communist takeover seemed imminent in both Western Europe and the Middle East.

Almost a year earlier Winston Churchill in a speech at Fulton, Missouri, with President Truman present, had appealed for a 'special relationship' between Britain and the United States for 'the sure prevention of war'. At this time there had been no favourable response, but now America reacted quickly. On 12 March Truman asked Congress for immediate financial and military aid for Turkey and Greece as part of a general policy of the 'containment' of communism in all countries threatened by Communist invasion or revolt.

Assistance [he stated] is imperative. . . . It must be the policy of the U.S.A. to support free peoples . . . resisting . . . armed minorities or . . . outside pressure. . . . The

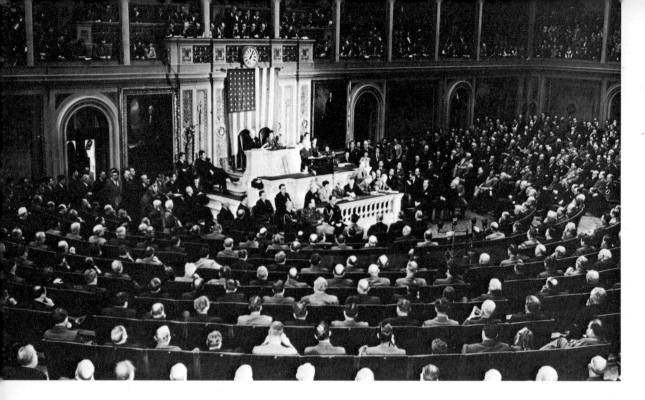

20 12 March 1947. President Truman, in a historic
speech, asks Congress for aid for Greece and Turkey

free peoples of the world look to us for support. . . . If we falter in our leadership we may
endanger the peace of the world and shall surely endanger the welfare of our own
nation. . . .[1]

The 'Truman Doctrine' had been announced and the 'Age of Containment' had
begun. $400 million were immediately voted to aid Greece and Turkey and military
missions were despatched to them. America had finally emerged from her isolationism
to take command of the 'Free World' in a Cold War which has already lasted longer than
the two world wars combined. Unfortunately, she was often to champion against
communism governments of a doubtful democratic nature and into this category fell
the existing régimes in Turkey and Greece.

In March 1947 America was still the only nation with the atomic bomb. Russian
cities were as open to destruction as Hiroshima and Nagasaki had been and the tougher
American attitude only increased Russian fears of capitalist attack. Russia on the other
hand had a great superiority in conventional forces so that the Truman Doctrine
marked the beginning of a long period of international tension that was to spread from
Europe to Asia, Africa, Latin America, and the world at large.

America was first intent upon restoring stability to war-torn Western Europe to
stem the increasing spread of communism. Italy and France faced the prospect of starvation by the end of 1947 and Russia seemed to be waiting for them to fall into her
hands. In a speech at Harvard University on 5 June 1947 General George Marshall,
the American Secretary of State, therefore offered American aid to promote European

[1] Keesing's Contemporary Archives, pp. 8491-2.

30

recovery. It was emphasised that the aid should not be conditional, but that those nations who wished to receive it should decide for themselves how to use it in a programme of European Economic Recovery. Britain and France were quick to seize the offer and began to prepare the way for what in June 1948 became a 16-nation Organisation for European Recovery which was granted $22,400 million over a period of four years. The scheme was thrown open to Russia and her East European 'satellites', but after a brief meeting with the British and French Foreign Ministers Molotov refused and Marshall Aid was denounced as 'capitalist propaganda'.

Russia's reply to the Marshall Plan was immediately to tighten her hold over her East European buffer states who would have liked to benefit from American assistance. At the beginning of 1947 none of the satellites had been completely converted into states on the Russian model and the remnants of opposition parties still remained. Between 1947 and 1948, however, nationalism and all political opposition were crushed in a reign of terror, purges, and trials.

In Romania the National Peasant Party was banned in June 1947, and its leaders Iuliu Maniu and Ion Mihalache were imprisoned for life on a charge of conspiracy with America. The charge was possibly true, but in November 1947 the other opposition party, the Social Democrats, was merged with the Communists to form a United Workers' Party. King Michael was forced to abdicate and sovietisation was completed by Russian-style elections in March 1948. No opposition candidates stood. The government bloc, from which members were elected, was renamed the People's Democratic Front.

In Bulgaria the story was similar. The peasant leader, Petkov, was arrested in June 1947. Communist organisations and demonstrations called for his death and he was executed, despite British and American protests, three months later. The veteran socialist leader, Lulchev, was imprisoned for life. A new Soviet type of constitution followed and the socialists were absorbed by the Communists into a Fatherland Front.

Hungary, after the arrest of Bela Kovacs, followed the familiar pattern. Four parties sponsored candidates at the summer elections in 1947 when 35 per cent of the electorate still voted for the opposition. The Communist Rakosi, however, became vice-premier and all opposition, including that of the Catholic Church, was relentlessly crushed. The inevitable fusion of socialists and Communists came in June 1948. By the end of the year Communist control was complete and Hungary became another 'People's Democracy' with a Soviet constitution. Poland, which had obtained its Soviet constitution in February 1947, fell completely under Communist direction with the creation of the Polish United Workers' Party from the socialists and Communists in December 1948. Only Finland and Czechoslovakia remained. A Russo-Finnish military alliance was concluded in February 1948. The establishment of Communist control in Czechoslovakia, however, required harsher measures which brought to an end liberal democracy.

Czechoslovakia, despite its Communist government, was not yet fully absorbed into the Russian bloc. When Marshall Aid was announced its government decided unanimously to accept it. The Czech Prime Minister, Gottwald, and several other Ministers, were then called to Moscow where they were ordered to refuse. With support waning the Communists feared defeat in the elections scheduled for the spring of 1948. To counter this they began to pack the Prague police with Communists and strengthen their control of the army. Additional Russian units entered the Soviet zone of Austria and took up positions near the Czech border. In February 1948 a dozen liberal Ministers resigned in protest, hoping for the support of their President, Eduard Benes. Benes enjoyed great personal prestige and national support in Czechoslovakia. The liberals hoped he would refuse their resignations and cause the formation of a new government in their favour. They were doomed to disappointment. No support was forthcoming from the Social Democrats and with their aid the Communists had a slender majority and a claim to form a new government.

Benes was in ill health and was badly advised. Like many Czechs he was still strongly influenced by the Munich betrayal of 1938. He did not believe that the Communists would destroy democracy and looked to the Russians as fellow Slavs to protect Czechoslovakia from the horrors of another German occupation in the future. He therefore re-appointed Gottwald in a government in which Communists predominated. Meanwhile armed Communist workers demonstrated in Prague; Communist strikes occurred in the major industries and Action Committees sprang up in the provinces. The democratic Ministers were replaced and their party newspapers suppressed. Jan Masaryk, Benes' lieutenant, and son of the founder of the Czech national state, died in mysterious circumstances. Once again Communists and Social Democrats amalgamated and a new constitution was proclaimed on Soviet lines. Benes, tired and disillusioned, refused to sign the new constitution and resigned in June 1948. He died six months later. The vast multitude at his funeral was a silent protest against the new régime established by the February *coup*.

In Western Europe Russian reaction to the Marshall Plan was equally violent. Here, national Communist parties directed by Moscow attempted to stop economic recovery by a series of violent strikes. The Communists were assisted in their task by cold, hunger, and widespread hardship and discontent. In Britain, economic dislocation took the form of unofficial coal strikes and stoppages in the docks. In France, where the Communists were stronger, and where Premier Ramadier had dismissed four Communist Ministers in May 1947, the disturbances were more serious. Strikes of miners and Paris transport-workers were followed by protest strikes at the reduction of the bread ration. In November 1947 the movement culminated in building and engineering strikes, a series of municipal strikes, and widespread transport strikes. Communist-led riots broke out in Marseilles. With 2 million workers idle coal and food supplies

21   President Benes arrives on a visit to Moscow. *On far left*, Vyshinsky; *next to President*, Molotov, Russian Foreign Minister

22   Jan Masaryk, Czech Foreign Minister (*front row, right*) and colleagues listen to a speech by Benes on the eve of the Communist takeover

collapsed. Starvation seemed imminent: Ramadier resigned and his government was replaced by that of Robert Schuman which was pledged to prevent civil war. By December, however, the strikers were tiring of Communist leadership and the strikes collapsed. Communist newspapers were closed and party activities suppressed. There were further disorders and rail sabotage in early 1948 but Communist support was waning and the prospect of revolution had gone. Communist pledges of support to Russia and the Red Army had offended French patriotism and henceforth the strength of French communism declined.

Italy underwent a similar crisis. Cost-of-living protest strikes in July 1947 had been transformed by October into farm strikes, hunger demonstrations, and a land seizure campaign. These coincided with strikes of metal- and textile-workers. After this, despite a newspaper strike and a general strike in Rome in April 1948, the influence of Palmiro Togliatti's Italian Communist Party weakened. This was due partly to strong government action and also to the emphasis of Italian communism upon Russian rather than national interests.

As Russia completed her ascendancy over Eastern Europe a conference of national Communist Party representatives at Warsaw established in October 1947 the Cominform, which was a revival of the Comintern dissolved in 1943. Its object was to co-ordinate activities and organise common defence and obedience in the Communist 'bloc' against American 'imperialism'. To the Russians, Marshall Aid was a means of reviving their old enemy, Germany, and replacing 'political imperialism' by 'economic imperialism'. Small nations receiving aid would be drawn into the Western trading system and would be expected to provide military, naval, and air bases to help in the encirclement of Russia. The new Cominform included representatives of Russia, Poland, Yugoslavia, Romania, Hungary, Bulgaria, Czechoslovakia, Italy, and France. Fears were soon aroused that its activities would stretch well beyond Europe since its formation was followed by outbreaks of Communist revolution in Malaya, Burma, Indonesia, and Indo-China.

In Western Europe those nations that had become associated with America through the receipt of Marshall Aid now felt themselves in grave danger of Russian attack. All that appeared to stand between a Russian invasion of defenceless Western

23 Matyas Rakosi, whose rule plunged Hungary into a reign of terror

24 Alcide De Gasperi, the great Italian statesman and Prime Minister who was mainly responsible for Italy's post-war recovery

Europe was the American possession of the atomic bomb. Conversely, all that stood between Russia and nuclear attack was the fact that her armies held Western Europe as a hostage. As the gulf between the two camps widened each appeared to the other to be intent upon world domination and any move towards greater security on the part of the one led to counter-measures on the part of the other.

The shock of the *coup* in Czechoslovakia and the formation of the Cominform hastened the conclusion in March 1948 of the Brussels treaty for collective security signed by Britain, France, Holland, Belgium, and Luxembourg. The treaty established permanent organisations for joint military action in the event of any armed aggression in Europe. It was the first Western alliance against Russian attack and as such was welcomed by America.

The total population of the Western bloc still outnumbered that of Russia's empire but there was an urgent need for rearmament and remobilisation. On the day that the Brussels treaty was signed America reintroduced measures for conscription. Congress also authorised heavy expenditure to increase American air power and begin a large-scale programme of nuclear research. Work also began with Canada for the establishment of an 'early warning' system across the polar regions as a safeguard against sudden Russian air attack (see Map 8). Rearmament programmes also began in Britain and France.

By mid-1948 liberal democracy had been replaced throughout Eastern Europe by Communist People's Democracies subservient to Russia and hostile to the West. The sole exception was Yugoslavia where Russia's attempts to increase her hold on the Eastern bloc led to an open rift. Tito had supported Russia on all major issues between 1945 and 1948, and had joined the Cominform in 1947. His régime, however, owed nothing to Soviet support but was based upon the war-time success of his partisans and his own brand of national communism. He had no reason for gratitude or subservience to Stalin and refused to accept Soviet orders which were contrary to Yugoslavia's national interests. Russia's objection to Yugoslav attempts to absorb Albania strained the relationship still further. Tito was regarded as too independent and therefore unreliable. He dared to criticise Moscow on minor matters and in June 1948 was expelled from the Cominform which called for his overthrow. Yugoslav Communists, however, remained loyal to him and he successfully weathered Russian threats and economic attacks. Yugoslavia, although remaining a Communist state, became a neutral in the Cold War as the withdrawal of Russian technical and economic aid forced her to accept help offered by America.

Tito's unexpected behaviour resulted in a campaign in the Eastern European states against other potential 'deviators' who might place national before purely Russian interests. Gomulka, Secretary of the Polish Communist Party, was denounced in September 1948. Kostov, his Bulgarian counterpart, was executed in 1949 and a similar fate befell native Communist leaders in Albania and Hungary. A further result of Tito's breach with Stalin was the end of the Communist revolution in Greece which had never received Russian support. In July 1949 Tito closed the Yugoslav frontier with Greece and deprived the Communists of a major source of support. Their cause was already wavering. It now completely collapsed, and the rebels fled into Albania. British troops were finally withdrawn that winter, and a moderate government elected in March 1950 began the task of reconstruction. Communism had been contained in Greece but by this time the sources of tension had switched elsewhere.

4 The Berlin Blockade and NATO

IN GERMANY, where the Western allies were still intent upon promoting German unity and recovery, the British and American zones were merged in January 1947, and were joined by the French in mid-1948. The benefits of this amalgamation could not be reaped without a reform of the German currency to check the ever-increasing prices. The Russians were invited to take part in a currency reform throughout the whole of Germany, but refused when the Western powers would not allow them to print their own notes. The West feared they would overprint and renew the inflation, and so decided to proceed alone. It was also agreed to apply the European Recovery Programme to the Western zones, and a federal constitution was proposed for western Germany.

Russia, however, was still determined to dominate Germany by keeping her poor. A prosperous West Germany would have a bad effect upon the impoverished East German zone, and might also eventually try to regain her lost territories to the east. The Russian reply, therefore, was an attempt to force the Western powers from Berlin which lay 110 miles inside the Russian zone (see Map 2). If this succeeded it would destroy West German confidence in the West and end the plans for West German recovery and a federal government.

On 20 March 1948 the Russians walked out of the Control Council. Ten days later new regulations were introduced for halting and inspecting traffic, and Russian harassing tactics on the road and railway routes between Berlin and the Western zones began. The American General Clay tried to insist upon Western access rights to Berlin and to refuse Russian inspection of Western vehicles. A 'test' train of American soldiers was, however, shunted into a siding and eventually obliged to return. Passenger trains were next refused permission to leave Berlin for West Germany. Gradually

25   August 1948. A U.S. Air Force C-47 Globemaster
is unloaded at Gatow airport, while a Dakota comes in
to land

35

Russian controls were tightened until on 24 June, four days after the introduction of Western currency reform, all road, rail, and canal traffic between Berlin and the West ground to a halt. 'Technical difficulties' such as repairs to canal sluices, the Elbe autobahn bridge, and the Berlin–Helmstedt railway (see Map 3), had forced the Soviet authorities to close them 'for a long period of time'. Simultaneously, all electricity obtained by West Berlin from the Russian zone was cut off.

No chance of negotiation existed in the city since the Russians had withdrawn from the Kommandatura. While the Russian Chief-of-Staff, Colonel Kalinin, denounced the new currency as an attempt to disorganise the economy of Berlin which was 'part of the economic system of the Soviet Zone', the Western sectors were in a state of total ground blockade. Supplies of food and fuel for their $2\frac{1}{2}$ million people existed for only six weeks. The Russian action was virtually an act of war. The Western powers could fully appreciate its importance when they remembered the Munich Agreement with Hitler in 1938.

'When Berlin falls', stated General Clay, 'Western Germany will be next. . . . If we withdraw our position in Berlin, Europe is threatened. . . . Communism will run rampant.'[1]

While they were united in their determination to stay in Berlin, they were un-decided how to meet the challenge. Britain was prepared to break through the blockade with tanks in the belief that Russia would not risk a war. France was not. When America calculated it would take 18 months before her ground forces could equal those of Russia the risks of open conflict were obviously too great. No mention was made of the atomic bomb but 60 American long-range bombers were quickly moved to bases in the British Isles. Only the Americans General Clay and Colonel Howley at first saw that the Berlin situation could be saved by means of a massive airlift supplying the Western sectors with fuel, food, clothing, and raw materials. When President Truman adopted Clay's suggestion on 24 June 1948, it was regarded by many as a temporary measure which would provide a breathing space for negotiation.

By the end of June a fleet of American aircraft from Frankfurt and Wiesbaden, and R.A.F. transport planes from Hanover, were operating a daily food service to Berlin. 125 American and 100 British planes landed at Berlin's Tempelhof and Gatow airports on 30 June (see Map 3). This number had increased to 280 American and 235 British aircraft by 18 July. The French, handicapped by shortage of planes, were able to make only a small contribution. Cargoes of coal in preparation for the winter were brought in for the first time by American planes on 7 July. Their progress did not go unhindered by the Russians who 'buzzed' Western planes and carried out air-to-air

[1] General L. Clay, *Division in Germany* (Heinemann), p. 361.

26 Frankfurt airport,
West Germany. U.S.
planes line up to fly off
with more provisions
for besieged Berlin

36

MAP NO. 3 THE BERLIN BLOCKADE (1948)

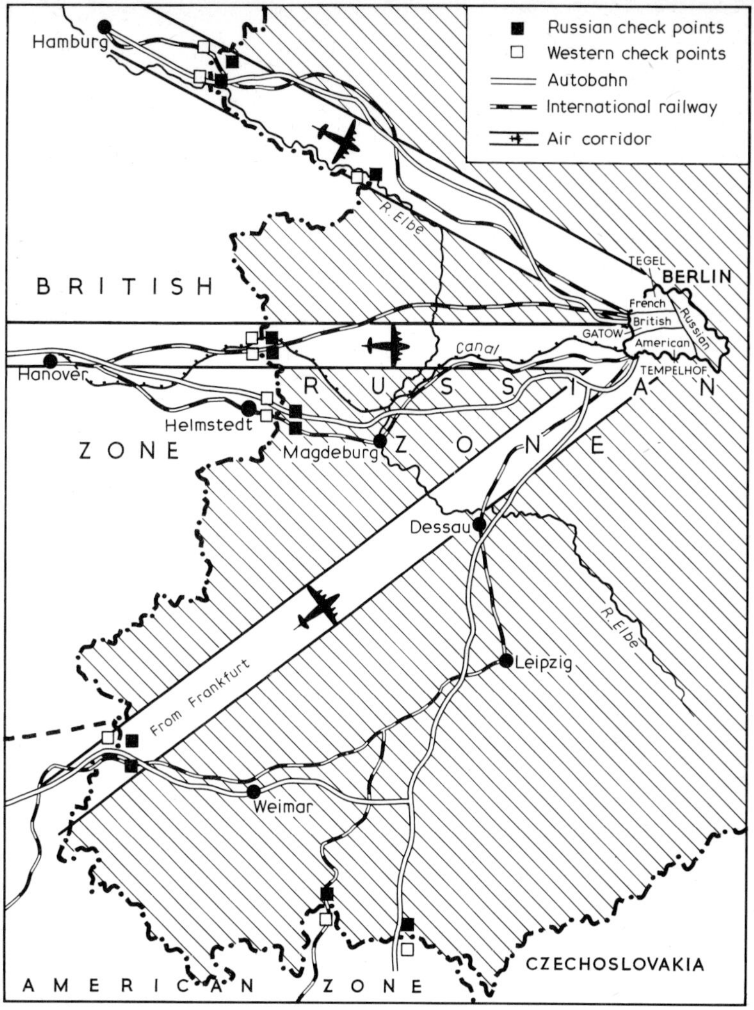

Russian check points
Western check points
Autobahn
International railway
Air corridor
Hamburg
R. Elbe
BRITISH
ZONE
TEGEL
BERLIN
French
British
American
Russian
GATOW
TEMPELHOF
Canal
Hanover
Helmstedt
Magdeburg
RUSSIAN
ZONE
Dessau
R. Elbe
Leipzig
From Frankfurt
Weimar
CZECHOSLOVAKIA
AMERICAN ZONE

and air-to-ground practice firing near the air corridors. Nevertheless, by the close of July, the airlift had increased its carriage from 2,000 to 4,000 tons a day, and the cancellation of plans for the demobilisation of 2,400 R.A.F. personnel indicated that the Western powers were beginning to resign themselves to a protracted trial of strength. On 26 July, when negotiations had proved fruitless, the West had launched its own counter-blockade with a ban on goods transport to the Soviet zone intended to create a shortage of raw materials in eastern Germany.

The morale of the West Berlin population, despite its peril in this tense conflict between its recent conquerors, remained high. From the outset the majority were determined to resist a Russian takeover by 'a campaign of starvation'. After refusing transport of a large consignment of Czechoslovakian potatoes and Polish coal to West Berlin, the Russians offered to feed West Berliners themselves provided that they purchased their rations in the Russian sector. Only a tiny minority accepted the offer and a violent clash between West Berliners and East German police and Soviet troops was narrowly avoided in early September. Impassioned West Berliners ripped down and burned the Russian flag at the Brandenburg Gate just inside the Soviet zone. East German police vehicles were overturned and Russian troops fired on the crowd. Only the separation of the two sides by British soldiers prevented a menacing riot.

Meanwhile preparation continued for the crucial winter ahead. By 30 September, the hundredth day of the blockade, 140,000 tons of coal, 104,000 tons of food, and 6,000 tons of other goods, apart from those needed by Western forces personnel, had been brought into Berlin. On 15 October the U.S.A.F. and R.A.F. groups concerned in the airlift were merged into a Combined Air Lift Task Force. A third airport at Tegel in the French zone, built in three months, was opened on 5 November. The tower of Radio Berlin, which was in Russian hands but in the French sector, and which hampered this airport's effectiveness, was blown up. At the other West Berlin airports radar and sodium lighting were installed to permit landings in fog. Sick and undernourished children were evacuated from the city.

To save coal each household was rationed to 25 lb. a month. To conserve electricity there were no tram, trolley-bus, or underground services between 6.00 p.m. and 6.00 a.m. Street lighting was reduced and the consumption of domestic electricity limited to two hours in the morning and evening. There was also a cut in gas supplies and an 80 per cent reduction in industrial current. Waste of fuel, gas, and electricity became a punishable offence. Throughout a bitter winter in which there were as many as 30 degrees of frost West Berliners shared each other's kitchens and strictly kept the rule that only alternate trees in the streets should be chopped down for firewood. As the airlift visibly increased in scale their resistance was maintained.

By 26 December, after six months in the air, Western planes had made 96,640 flights, an average of 552 flights a day, and brought in over 700,000 tons of food, coal, raw materials, and manufactured goods. By the spring an average of 8,000 tons, including 5,000 tons of coal, was being delivered daily, a feat described by Clement Attlee, the British Prime Minister, who visited West Berlin in March 1949, as 'one of the wonders of the world'. On 16 April 1,398 planes landed the record amount of 13,000 tons, the equivalent of 22 freight trains with 50 carriages each. Aircraft at Tempelhof were landing and taking off at the rate of one a minute, and more goods were entering West Berlin than before the blockade. It was clear that Russia could not drive the West from Germany nor change its policy there without a full-scale war. To stop the airlift, Stalin had to shoot down Western planes, and this he would not do out of fear of American nuclear weapons. The tremendous expense and effort of 'Operation Vittles' had won a Western victory.

27 British troops and German civilians unload supplies at Gatow airport

On 27 January 1949 Stalin hinted that he was ready to reconsider his terms for raising the Berlin blockade. Finally at midnight on 12 May 1949 British and American vehicles crossed the frontiers of the Soviet zone and proceeded to Berlin without interference. After ten and a half months the blockade had been beaten by 'the most outstanding transport operation in the history of aviation'. The airlift continued until 30 September when stocks in Berlin were sufficient to meet any sudden renewal of the blockade. In all about 2·3 million tons of goods were landed in Berlin. Two-thirds of this amount was carried by the U.S.A.F. and the remainder by the R.A.F. 36 American planes were lost and 79 American, British, and German pilots and ground staff died in accidents. Apart from the human and material cost the price of the Western victory was the complete separation of the Soviet and Western zones and the appearance of two Berlins – East Berlin, firmly planted in the Communist zone, and West Berlin, isolated from western Germany, which lay over a hundred miles to the west.

At the height of the Berlin crisis in September 1948 General Clay had confidently stated to journalists that he had 'no reason to believe war is just around the corner'. There is no doubt, however, that one incident or accident during these anxious months could have plunged the world into a Third World War. Memories of the years before 1939, revived by the blockade, drove many Western nations to the conclusion that they must resist the spread of communism from a position of strength. The result on 4 April 1949 was the signing by the United States, Canada, and ten European powers of the North Atlantic Pact which created the defensive alliance of the North Atlantic Treaty Organisation (NATO). In addition to the five Brussels treaty powers of Britain, France, Belgium, Holland, and Luxembourg, the treaty was also signed in Washington by Italy, Portugal, Iceland, Denmark, and Norway. Portugal was intended as a strategic bridgehead for the United States if Russia should sweep westwards across mainland Europe to the Bay of Biscay. Italy was intended to act as a barrier against Communist advance through the Mediterranean (see Map 4).

The alliance was planned to last initially for 20 years. It created a North Atlantic Council and an Executive Committee of Foreign Ministers who were to meet at least annually. It also established a Defence Council of War Ministers and a Committee of Chiefs of Staff. Its headquarters were situated at the Palais de Chaillot in Paris with a Secretary-General and an international staff. The purpose of the organisation was to keep the peace by resisting aggression within the framework of the United Nations. An initial grant of $1,000 million was made to members by America so that they could begin rearmament. America, Britain, and Canada agreed to keep armed forces in Europe under the command of General Eisenhower who became NATO's first Supreme Commander until he was elected American President in 1952.

A month after the North Atlantic Treaty was signed the three Western zones of Germany became the (West) German Federal Republic with its capital at Bonn. In the same month, after a Russian-style constitution had been accepted by the people of East Germany, the Soviet zone became the (East) German Democratic Republic. Thus by mid-1949 two republics existed in Germany, the one sponsored by the Western powers and the other by Soviet Russia. Neither would recognise the state that the other had created. The West claimed that only the Russian refusal to permit free East German elections prevented complete German unification. The Russians saw the creation of the Federal Republic as a step towards the renewal of German aggression against Russia.

In mid-1949 the twelve NATO powers could raise under 3 million men as opposed to the Soviet army of over 4 million and its air force of 20,000 planes. Russian divisions

39

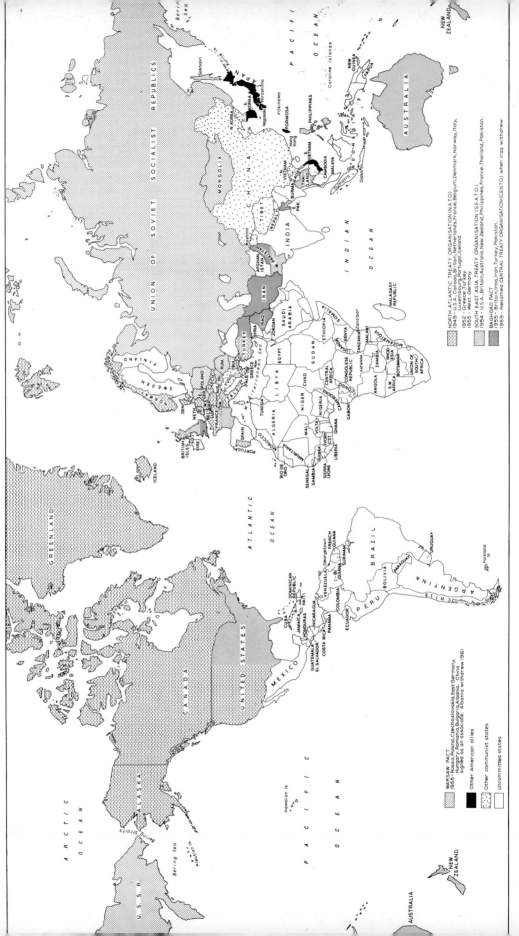

MAP NO. 4   THE WORLD OF THE COLD WAR

28 Dean Acheson, U.S. Secretary of State, signs the North Atlantic Treaty. Behind him is President Truman and behind Truman the British Foreign Secretary Ernest Bevin (wearing spectacles)

along the Iron Curtain outnumbered the NATO divisions by 125 to 14 and later by 263 to 175. Had the Russians desired it the flimsy NATO ground forces could, at this time, have been swept aside. NATO strategy was based upon 'the Sword and the Shield'. The 'Shield' represented the small NATO army, supplied mainly by its European members, whose task was to delay any Russian advance into Western Europe long enough for the 'Sword' to be brought into action. The 'Sword' was the atomic bomb which could be dropped upon Russia from America's NATO and Pacific bases.

Russia, however, after four frantic years of research, possessed the atomic bomb by late 1949 although her stockpile was doubtless smaller than that of America. If anything it was uncertainty of her own East European satellites as much as fear of the nuclear strength of NATO which prevented a Russian advance into Western Europe between 1949 and 1950 before NATO rearmament had really got under way. If she attacked, her lines of communication lay through unreliable satellites who might be tempted to cut them. The Russian response in Europe therefore to the creation of NATO was to increase her grip upon the Peoples' Democracies. Political purges took place in Hungary, Bulgaria, Albania, Poland, and Czechoslovakia, and leaders of the Catholic Church who threatened to undermine Communist influence in Eastern Europe were savagely attacked. A Russian 'Peace Offensive', too, was launched in an attempt to win the support of those in the NATO powers and the uncommitted countries who were genuinely repelled by the prospects of nuclear warfare.

The strategy of the 'Sword and the Shield' was largely intended to give confidence to the peoples of Western Europe. Many Western Europeans were at first openly cynical about the part which they had to play in it. Gradually, however, the success of the airlift and the growth of NATO helped to quell the awful feeling of insecurity in Europe which had existed since 1945. As Western Europe and America drew more closely together and NATO provided a balance to the enormous Russian armies in Eastern Europe the feeling that war was inevitable began to fade. The West was soon, however, to discover that it required a stronger 'Shield' of conventional forces as the Cold War moved from Europe to the Far East with Communist success in the Chinese revolution, the spread of communism in Asia, and the outbreak of the Korean war.

5 The Communist Conquest of China

IN JAPAN THE SPREAD of post-war communism was successfully prevented by America's exclusion of Russia, her revival of Japanese industry, and land reforms. American occupation was ended by the San Francisco treaty of 1951 by which the Emperor was reduced to a figurehead and Japan became a democracy without armed forces. A Security Pact was signed with America in the same year.

American efforts to produce, by peaceful settlement, a similar post-war democracy in China failed disastrously. The divisions in Chinese society were far too deep. Since 1927, the Kuomintang, General Chiang Kai-Shek's Chinese Nationalist Party, had been locked in bitter conflict with the Chinese Communists. Chiang had almost destroyed the Communists in 1934, but some 40,000 had survived a Long March of 6,000 miles from their original stronghold in Kiangsi in south-east China, to establish a new base at Shensi in the north-west (see Map 5). By 1936 their leader, Mao Tse-Tung, was ruler of 10 million people. The Japanese invasion of 1936 brought an uneasy truce between the rival factions which temporarily united against the common enemy. The Japanese war allowed the Communists to extend their influence throughout north-east China. As Nationalist troops retreated they infiltrated behind Japanese lines, organised resistance, and administered these 'liberated areas' where land was distributed among the peasants. By March 1944 64 per cent of the Japanese forces in China were operating against the Communists behind their lines. Such was Chiang's distrust of his allies that while the Japanese pressed southwards, seriously defeating the Nationalists, he kept several hundred thousand of his best troops ringing the Communist border region to prevent the extension of the Communist zone. Nevertheless, by the Japanese surrender the Communists controlled almost 400,000 square miles of territory in the northern border region. Their regular armies, the 8th Route Army of the border region and the 4th Army of the Yangtse Valley, numbered some 470,000 men in addition to a further 2 million guerrillas.

The Communists hoped to keep control of the provinces they had liberated, leaving the remainder to the Nationalists and relying upon peaceful propaganda for the eventual spread of communism throughout China. The Kuomintang government, dominated by corrupt landowners, businessmen, and financiers, was democratic neither in form nor profession. It was determined to use the modern armaments obtained during the war from America finally to stamp out communism. Negotiations during 1944 intended to settle differences between Nationalists and Communists broke down. The Communists demanded the immediate establishment of democracy, freedom of speech, and local self-government together with recognition of the Communist Party. These the Nationalists refused, demanding instead that the Communist armies should be reduced and absorbed into the Nationalist army, a factor which only increased Communist suspicion of the Nationalist leaders. During 1944 each side had accused the other of unwarranted attacks. The Japanese surrender on 12 August 1945 was the signal for a race to seize strategic positions. In north China the Communist commander Chu Teh, a former soldier of the Imperial army, launched an all-out offensive against the Japanese, intending to occupy their positions and seize their arms. This

29   Mao Tse-Tung with his
Commander-in-Chief, Chu Teh

30   Chiang Kai-Shek on a visit to
officers of the 14th U.S. Army

had been expressly forbidden by Chiang Kai-Shek who insisted that the Kuomintang
government should make arrangements for the Japanese surrender. In this way the
Communists would be excluded from the peace settlement and the chance to secure
weapons.

As civil war drew nearer Mao Tse-Tung and his adviser on foreign affairs, Chou
En-Lai, travelled on 28 August to Chungking for further negotiations. They were
accompanied by the American ambassador who acted as a mediator in an attempt to
keep the peace. Their journey was prompted by the news that Russia had signed a
treaty with the Nationalists in which she recognised Chiang's régime as the legal government of China. After six weeks of negotiation no decision was reached regarding either
the future of the Communist army or the question of control in north China. While the
negotiations were in progress further fighting broke out in central and northern China
between the Communists and the Nationalists and Japanese. The latter had been
instructed by the American General MacArthur to surrender only to the Kuomintang
south of the Great Wall and to Russia in Manchuria.

Faced with superior opposition the Communists began to evacuate the area south
of the Yangtse and concentrate their forces in north China. It might have been wise for
Chiang to consolidate his position south of the Yangtse and to try to win the support of
China's 80 per cent peasant population by agrarian reforms before moving north
against the Communists. South China, however, was a poor food-producing area.
North China was more fertile and Manchuria, developed by the Japanese, was a great
industrial area rich in coal and iron. The need to 'save face' plus economic necessity
meant that Chiang had to secure north China and beat the Communists into Manchuria
where they hoped to take over from the Russians. His bases, however, lay far to the south,
and this policy eventually proved his undoing.

As the retreating Communists were destroying the railways to the north, Chiang
turned to the Americans, who had already equipped his armies, for further aid. When
by 13 September the Kuomintang had occupied Nanking, Shanghai, and Hankow, the

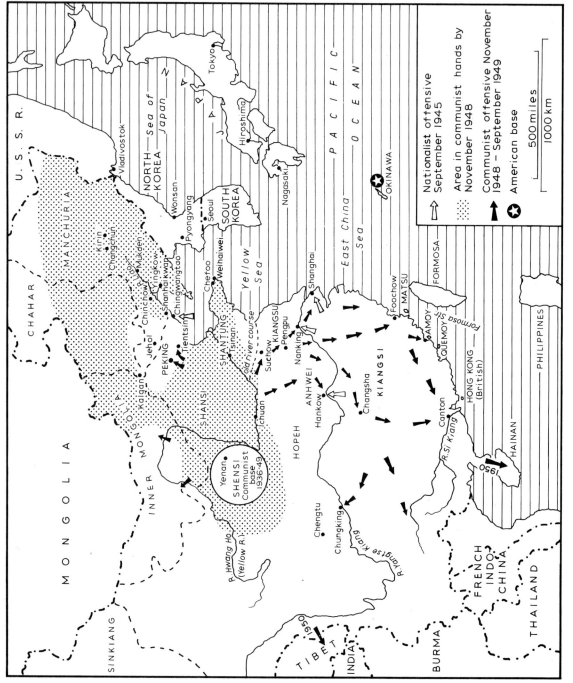

MAP NO. 5
THE COMMUNIST CONQUEST OF CHINA

44

U.S. 10th Air Force with 235 planes rapidly flew two Nationalist armies to Peking to establish control of the north. In Manchuria, however, the Russians as they withdrew handed the area and its Japanese arms dumps to the Communists. With the Communists controlling the Manchurian ports and the approaches by land the Nationalists seemed shut out from this rich province. On 1 November, however, the U.S. 7th Fleet landed two Nationalist armies at Chingwangtao at the eastern end of the Great Wall. These stormed the old walled town of Shanhaikwan with the aid of tanks and artillery and bursting through the Great Wall fanned out into Manchuria. By 21 November they had penetrated 80 miles into Manchuria while other Nationalist forces took the Nankow Pass and entered Jehol (see Map 5). At this stage the Russians decided Mao's cause was lost. Further help was withheld in this sphere as Stalin was not prepared for a direct clash with America. Meanwhile American Lease-Lend Aid continued to equip a further 39 of Chiang's divisions and provide him with eight air groups.

After the Nationalist entry into Manchuria the civil war temporarily halted. The pause coincided with the arrival on 23 December 1945 of the American General George Marshall charged with the unenviable task of again mediating between the two parties. Hopes ran high when both sides agreed to a truce on 14 January 1946, and negotiations again commenced. Tension was soon renewed, however, as the Russians, having removed all the Japanese industrial machinery, began to depart from Manchuria. When they left Mukden on 11 March the Communists occupied the city but were driven out by Nationalists the following day. On 19 April, again as the Russians left Changchun, the Manchurian capital was seized by Red forces only to be retaken by the Kuomintang on 23 May. In vain Marshall tried to mediate. A cease-fire, negotiated on 6 June, was prolonged until 13 June. In the first week in July it broke down and heavy fighting spread through north China. In an effort to convince the Communists of his good faith Marshall secured a ban on the shipment of British and American arms to the Kuomintang government which lasted from July 1946 to May 1947, but Chiang already had ample reserves and was convinced that he could quickly decide the issue by force. He had every reason for confidence. His army of $2\frac{1}{2}$ million men by far outclassed his enemies in numbers and equipment. He had also a small navy and air force again provided by the Americans. His opponent, Mao, had neither navy nor air force; his army, though increasing, was only partially equipped with firearms. In contrast to Chiang, one of the 'Big Four', supported by the world's most powerful state, Mao ruled only a small territory without money, resources, or allies. Russia, his only possible ally, had abandoned him as lost. Few foreign observers predicted anything but a speedy and decisive victory for Chiang when the civil war recommenced and the Nationalists took the province of Jehol and cleared Kiangsu of Red forces in early September 1946. The fall of Kalgan, the capital of Chahar and most important Communist centre outside Yenan, followed on 13 October. On 20 November Chou En-Lai, after spending almost a year in Nationalist China trying with Marshall and the Kuomintang to find a formula to solve the crisis, flew back to the Communist capital of Yenan. Marshall's mission had proved a failure and on 8 January 1947 he too returned home. He left the Nationalists engaged in a gigantic project to divert the Yellow river eastward into its former course. If successful this would have flooded Anhwei and Kiangsu, destroyed the livelihood of thousands, and left a vast mud flat isolating the Communist forces in Shantung from those in Hopeh (see Map 5). The project was abandoned, but during the first half of 1947 Chiang's armies continued to try by more orthodox military

45

methods to split up the Communist zones in north China. To raise Nationalist prestige an attack was also launched upon Yenan.

At first this strategy seemed to meet with some success. Linyi, the Communists' headquarters in Shantung, fell on 3 February 1947. Another Nationalist offensive at the beginning of March was reported to have trapped 60,000 Communists and annihilated 20,000 others, and on 19 March Yenan, the Red capital for eleven years, was occupied by the Kuomintang. It had already been abandoned by the Communists who had long expected this attack and had moved their seat of government to Shansi.

While the capture of Yenan was hailed as a Nationalist triumph, Chiang's situation was by no means as secure as it appeared. The Communists' withdrawal from southern and central China had concentrated their forces; the Nationalist armies were widely and dangerously scattered in areas where supply was difficult. Three-quarters of

31   Communist troops on the march

32   Sheltered by trenches, Chinese Communist troops shell the walls of the capital of Shansi province

Chiang's budget was being spent upon the war yet only a quarter of this amount was being raised by taxation. Prices during 1946 rose therefore by 700 per cent. While corruption was rampant in every section of the Kuomintang government service, Chiang's troops were underfed, ill-disciplined, poorly paid, and badly led. Their morale was crumbling and many were ready for desertion when the time came.

The initial Nationalist superiority had forced the Communists to continue the guerrilla warfare devised by Mao Tse-Tung and long practised against the Japanese. This consisted of lightning raids on garrisons and isolated units and rapid retreat from large-scale open conflict. Their main aims were to inflict greater losses upon the enemy than they themselves sustained and even more important to capture from their enemies the maximum amount of modern weapons. In both they were remarkably successful. A French correspondent writing in April 1947 reported that:

46

The capture of Houma cost the Reds 200 killed and wounded but brought them 1,800 prisoners. . . . The Nationalists do not bother to destroy their weapons before they surrender. . . . The lack of fighting spirit shown by the common soldier demonstrates the degree to which the Nationalist army has disintegrated. . . . Their troops do not want to fight. . . . The American aid they get ends . . . in the hands of the Communists. . . .[1]

By mid-1947 the Communist armies were beginning to make good their deficiencies in material and as they did so they began to abandon their guerrilla tactics and begin the large-scale offensive military operations which finally proved decisive. Their leadership, discipline, and morale were infinitely superior to that of the Nationalists. They had a cause which they believed worth fighting for and which constant political indoctrination saw that they understood. In this atmosphere Nationalist deserters were quickly converted into good Communist soldiers. The Communists had, moreover, the

33   Communist troops unload sandbags

support of the peasants. While Chiang ignored the question of land reform and his ill-disciplined soldiers plundered the peasantry, the Communists distributed the land among the peasants in the areas that they occupied. Communist soldiers when not fighting helped the peasants, upon whose goodwill they depended, in the fields. Communist instructors brought not terror but education and hygiene to the villages. China's population consisted of 80 per cent peasants, only 20 per cent of whom owned their own land. In the end their support would be decisive.

After the early Nationalist successes of 1947 came a series of Red counter-attacks. By May the Kuomintang was forced to admit that five towns in Shansi had been retaken by the Communists and four-fifths of the province was again in Red hands. By July half the Nationalist-occupied territory in Manchuria was lost together with vast quantities

[1] L. M. Chassin, *The Communist Conquest of China* (Weidenfeld & Nicolson), p. 113.

of arms and supplies as whole battalions deserted to the enemy. A 'general national mobilisation' of manpower and 'all commodities, foodstuffs, clothing, and medicine' was announced by the Nationalists on 4 July. Amphibious Nationalist landings at Chefoo and Weihaiwei in October helped to re-establish some Nationalist authority in Shantung but by the close of the year the whole of Manchuria, with the exception of the big cities of Mukden, Changchun, and Kirin, had fallen to the Communists. It would have paid Chiang better to withdraw his troops from Manchuria and concentrate them in north China. 'Loss of face' forbade this and so he kept his best troops buried in a distant land – which was eventually to prove his downfall.

On 1 January 1948, the Nationalist armies still outnumbered the Communists on paper by two to one but the Kuomintang was forced to admit losses of 400,000 for the year 1947, while Communist strength was still growing. In the first week of March the Nationalists suffered a major disaster at Ichuan, 60 miles south-east of Yenan, when their 29th Army was encircled by 80,000 Communist troops. Liu Chan, its commander, was killed and his army wiped out. By 31 March the Communists had recaptured Yenan and the Nationalists had withdrawn from the Shantung ports. In vain the American Congress voted aid of $125 million. It was too late. Two further major Communist offensives followed in September. One was directed against the Shantung capital of Tsinan which fell on 25 September. The other was aimed at the Mukden–Tientsin railway which was Mukden's sole surviving link with north China. The capture of Chinchow by Lin Piao's 140,000 Communists on 15 October and the seizure of Changchun, the Manchurian capital, three days later severed Mukden from all help. The city had been under siege by Communist artillery since December 1947. The garrison of 200,000 with tanks and artillery could have broken out but its general could think only of defence. By the close of October hope of holding Manchuria was gone. Government officials were flown out of Mukden which surrendered on 1 November. The Nationalist army retreated from Mukden to Yingkow where it was evacuated by sea, but the loss of Manchuria had cost the Nationalists seven armies with all their weapons (see Map 5). By mid-1948 the Communists had at last achieved parity in both armaments and men, the bulk of their equipment having come from the Nationalists. The time had come to go on to the offensive and the war moved rapidly south as Chu Teh prepared to attack Nanking. The only remaining barrier to keep him from Nanking and the Yangtse was Suchow, which became the scene of one of the decisive battles in history.

Each army totalled 600,000 men but the Nationalists had the additional advantage of more tanks, artillery, and complete air support. Kuomintang morale, however, was poor, and its generals bent only on defence. The 65-day battle which raged from 5 November to 10 January was fought against a background of food riots in Nanking and Shanghai where curfews and martial law were imposed. On 11 November the Kuomintang, faced with a financial and economic crisis, was obliged to devalue China's currency. Two Nationalist generals and 23,000 men deserted to the Communists. Chiang's armies were encircled and destroyed. Suchow was abandoned on 1 December and when the battle ended on 10 January 600,000 men and their equipment were lost. The Communists could sweep on to Nanking and the Yangtse and the last Kuomintang chance was gone (see Map 5).

Chiang, re-elected President in April 1948, warned the nation to prepare for another eight years of war but declared that the Communists could never win the war in 60 years. The new Communist North China People's Government which met in

34 Communist troops take prisoners at bayonet point during heavy fighting around Shanghai

August, however, had seats significantly reserved for 'areas to be liberated in the future'. Martial law was declared throughout all Nationalist China except Formosa and the western provinces as the Reds by-passed Pengpu and headed for Nanking which had only 70,000 troops left for its defence. While Madame Chiang Kai-Shek flew to Washington in a fruitless bid to secure American intervention, disaster also struck the Nationalists in the north. On 18 December Communist forces reached the outskirts of Peking which was occupied on 22 January. Tientsin had already fallen a week before.

As the Nationalist cause collapsed the Kuomintang government disintegrated. China, weak and disrupted by years of war and revolution, was yearning for peace. On 3 January 1949 the Shanghai City Council appealed to Mao for a cease-fire without consulting the Nationalist government. Other overtures followed. On 20 January Chiang resigned the Presidency and flew to south China where although ostensibly retired he began to prepare further military resistance.

Attempted negotiations broke down when the Communists demanded the punishment of all war criminals, including Chiang himself, and required an unconditional surrender. The Nationalists were determined to prevent a Communist crossing of the Yangtse but the military situation was now reversed. The Communists had the superiority in numbers and on 20 April, supported by heavy artillery, one million troops crossed China's great river on a 400-mile front. Resistance was negligible. Nanking, already abandoned, was occupied on 23 April and by the close of the month Shanghai, China's greatest city, was virtually encircled. Inside Shanghai, where the population of 3 million was swollen by hundreds of thousands of refugees, many merchants were anxious to surrender. The presence of a great community of industrial workers created the fear of a Communist rising, while to make matters worse the currency had completely collapsed.

On 28 April Chiang flew into Shanghai and prophesied victory 'within three years'. He was optimistic. Hankow fell on 16 May and Shanghai on 27 May. In June the Nationalists began a naval blockade of the Red coastline which now stretched from the Liao river in Manchuria to the port of Foochow. The Nationalist air force, too, twice bombed Shanghai. It was all in vain. Changsha, centre of the 'rice bowl' area, surrendered on 5 August when the Nationalist commander defected with his entire army to the Communists. Foochow followed on 17 August and by the end of the month the Communists were under 20 miles from the Nationalists' capital of Canton. Chiang, who had now in practice reassumed the Kuomintang leadership, tried to form a Far Eastern Union of anti-Communist states including the Philippines and Syngman Rhee's South Korea. This too came to naught and preparations were begun to evacuate Canton to the Chinese war-time capital of Chungking. Large concentrations of Chiang's best troops were also moved to the island of Formosa which was obviously destined to become his centre of long-term resistance.

A disastrous fire started by the Communist underground in Chungking on 2 September hindered the process of Nationalist evacuation. 100,000 were left homeless and over 1,000 people trying to escape by jumping into the Yangtse were drowned. The Nationalists had lost the will to fight and in the closing months of 1949 like 'a hurricane blowing the leaves before it' the Red armies swept through the remaining provinces of mainland China (see Map 5).

In Inner Mongolia, after the desertion of six army commanders and their troops, the Nationalist governors handed over to the Communists on 19 September. The vast province of Sinkiang followed their example ten days later. The last Nationalist troops left Canton on 14 October having blown up their munitions dumps. Amoy, Chiang's embarkation port for Formosa, which had been desperately defended for a month, fell two days later as the last Nationalists withdrew in junks and small craft to the offshore islands. The entire coastline opposite Formosa was now in the hands of the Communists, who were separated from their enemies only by the 140-mile-wide Formosa Strait.

On 30 November the Nationalist government left Chungking for Chengtu, their third capital in two months. When this fell on 27 December they fled to Formosa by air. Mao Tse-Tung had already anticipated their departure when on 1 October 1949 he had proclaimed before a crowd of 200,000 in the Square of the Gate of Heavenly Peace at Peking the birth of the People's Republic of China. The new régime controlled the entire Chinese mainland with the exception of Tibet. This along with Chiang's islands of Formosa, Hainan, Matsu, and Quemoy, it regarded as part of continental China. Mao Tse-Tung, for whom most observers had forecast nothing but destruction four years earlier, had become ruler of 400 million people and the biggest Communist state in the world.

The new state was first recognised by Burma on 9 December. Other Asiatic nations quickly followed suit. Britain finally withdrew recognition from the Nationalists and gave it to the Communists on 6 January 1950. For this she was strongly criticised by Chiang Kai-Shek and by her ally America who refused to recognise the new China. The government of the largest world population thus remained unrepresented at the United Nations. In America there was severe criticism of the Truman government which had allowed a friendly China to be replaced by a hostile one. It was strongly felt that Chiang Kai-Shek had been given insufficient help. On the other hand while America attempted to mediate she had continued to supply Chiang with American weapons. Much of the Communist success was based upon widespread hatred of the European colonial powers who had exploited China for so long. The Communist bombardment of the British frigate *Amethyst* during the crossing of the Yangtse, was a sign that European influence in China was over. At the start of the war the Chinese Communists had held Marshall and the Americans in some regard. By the end of the war they were bitterly anti-American and in February 1950 signed a 30-year treaty of friendship with Russia. If America had contained communism in the West she had certainly not done so in the East.

Nor were Chinese Communist ambitions yet satisfied. In a New Year Message Mao declared the tasks of the Chinese People's Army for 1950 to be the 'liberation' of Hainan, Tibet, and Formosa. The first two objectives were easier than the last. On 17 April 1950 170 motorised junks landed with four infantry divisions on Hainan. The Nationalist garrison heavily outnumbered the invaders but was attacked from within by Communist guerrillas. In four days the Communists held the island, which would have been an excellent base for the promised Nationalist return to the mainland.

On 7 October 1950 the Chinese invaded the eastern part of Tibet which had broken from Chinese rule in 1911. Tibet was an ancient land isolated by the world's highest mountain ranges and ruled by a 'god king', the Dalai Lama. A third of its male population were Buddhist monks and it was powerless to resist. For a while the Chinese advance was held up by the snow-bound passes to the Tibetan plateau 12,000 feet above sea level, but in May 1951 the Tibetans recognised Chinese suzerainty and in September Chinese troops entered the Tibetan capital of Lhasa. China had restored her Imperial frontiers, controlled the 'roof of the world', and was dangerously near to India (see Map 5).

35　Mao Tse-Tung reviews his troops

36　Communist troops even marched through Sha Tau Kok, on Hongkong territory

37　1 October 1949. Mao Tse-Tung proclaims the People's Republic of China

51

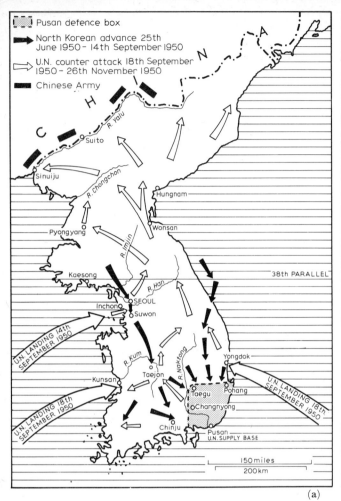

Pusan defence box

North Korean advance 25th June 1950 – 14th September 1950

U.N. counter attack 18th September 1950 – 26th November 1950

Chinese Army

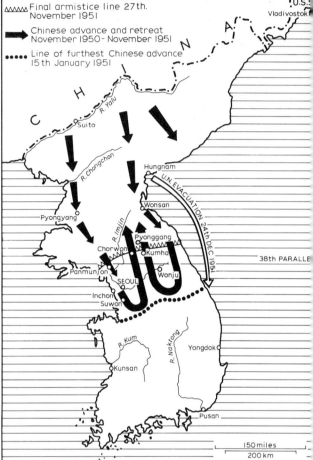

Final armistice line 27th. November 1951

Chinese advance and retreat November 1950 – November 1951

Line of furthest Chinese advance 15th January 1951

(a)

(b)

MAP NO. 6 (a) and (b)
THE KOREAN WAR, FIRST AND SECOND PHASES

38   July 1950. American troops on their way to the front pass a family of refugees

6 Limited War in Korea

WITH THE COMMUNIST victory in China the United States appeared to abandon Formosa and South Korea since they lay outside the American Pacific defence line which stretched from the Aleutian Islands through Japan and Okinawa to the Philippines. Korea, however, was a bridge between mainland China and Japan and the route by which forces from either might invade the other (see Map 8). At the close of the Pacific war the Korean peninsula, annexed by the Japanese in 1910, had been jointly occupied by Russia and America. The Russian zone lay to the north and the American zone to the south of the 38th parallel. The occupation was intended to last only while the Japanese were disarmed and the Koreans established their own independent national state. Like Germany, however, Korea soon became divided into two rival states. The Russians wished the new united Korea to be a Communist state while the Americans were equally determined that it should become a modern democracy.

When in September 1947 the Americans placed the question in the hands of the United Nations, the Russians refused to allow a U.N. Commission into their zone since they believed the U.N. was dominated by America. As the result of a general election in May 1948 a National Assembly was elected for South Korea which established a South Korean republic under the presidency of Dr Syngman Rhee, a Korean Nationalist. In response the Russians created a Communist People's Democratic Republic in North Korea led by Kim Il Sung who had served in the Russian army at Stalingrad. Russian forces withdrew from North Korea in December 1948; the Americans evacuated the South in June 1949. They left behind two mutually hostile governments. North Korea possessed the majority of Korea's industrial resources. South Korea held almost three-quarters of Korea's population. Both governments were determined to secure a united Korea under their own control, and border raids began.

In 1949 Syngman Rhee, whose democratic government soon proved suspect, boasted that he could take the Northern capital of Pyongyang in a few days. The American government, fearing that he might take aggressive action, kept him short of military supplies while North Korea, equipped by Russia, grew steadily stronger. To Stalin Korea, which America had apparently abandoned, undoubtedly seemed a fruitful field in which to make up for the failure of the Berlin blockade. In the early hours of 25 June 1950, spear-headed by Russian-built tanks and supported by Soviet Yak fighters, the North Korean army crossed the 38th parallel, captured the rail centre of Kaesong, crossed the Imjin river, and headed towards the southern capital of Seoul. Simultaneously North Korean seaborne landings took place on the east coast of South Korea. The South Korean troops, without armoured support, were brushed aside. The North Koreans claimed that their offensive was a retaliation for an attempted invasion of North Korea by the South (see Map 6a).

In Washington the news had the same impact as the Japanese onslaught on Pearl Harbor in December 1941. It was widely feared that a Chinese invasion of Formosa was due to coincide with the North Korean attack. If the Communists succeeded in Formosa and Korea they would then be face to face with America's Pacific defences. Moreover, the similarity between Hitler's aggression in Europe before 1939 and the events in Korea was strong. If the Communists were not stopped their aggression would continue, ending in a Third World War.

Meeting on the afternoon of 25 June at America's request the U.N. Security Council called for a cease-fire and the withdrawal of the North Koreans. A second meeting on the evening of 27 June promised to 'furnish such assistance to the Republic of Korea as may be necessary to repel the armed attack and to restore international peace and security in the area'. There was no Russian veto as the Russian delegate had been absent since January in protest against the U.N. refusal to give the Chinese seat in the Security Council to the new Communist China.

Before the resolution was passed, however, America had already acted. Telegrams from the United Nations Commission in Korea warned that the American-trained South Korean army was no match for the Korean People's Army created from anti-Japanese resistance groups and a volunteer corps which had fought for Mao Tse-Tung in Manchuria. At noon on 27 June with South Korea on the verge of collapse President Truman ordered support from American air and sea forces to be given to the South Korean armies. American forces were strengthened in the Philippines and the 7th Fleet was directed to the Formosa Strait to defend Formosa against Chinese invasion. Offers of help quickly followed from other nations who felt that if the U.N. failed to take action, as the League of Nations had done when Japan attacked China in 1931, it would perish in the same fashion. Australia immediately made available its Pacific warships and fighter squadrons in Japan, and Canada sent destroyers. Chiang Kai-Shek, quick to seize an opportunity to regain full American support, offered the assistance of 33,000 'seasoned' troops but was advised to keep them in Formosa.

Air and naval support alone was soon shown to be insufficient. Seoul fell on 28 June together with the nearby Kimpo airfield, and the Rhee government retired to Taejon. By 30 June the Communists had broken the South's Han river defence line by ferrying tanks across under cover of darkness and were pressing towards Suwon. As they advanced, the first American troops hurriedly left Japan for Korea by air. They included anti-tank gunners with armour-piercing 'bazookas', shoulder-fired rockets each operated by two men, and intended to stop the North Korean tanks. Landing at Pusan, the port nearest Japan, they were rushed north to meet the North Koreans.

39 A South Korean soldier talks to the homeless in bombed Pohang

40 American troops move up to the front from Taegu

Their arrival had little immediate effect. While monsoon rains hindered air operations Suwon was taken on 4 July. The build-up of American forces through Pusan was slow. Bad roads and the existence of only one inefficient railway from Pusan hindered their despatch to the front. The two best airports were already in Communist hands. Not only were flying conditions poor but American combat aircraft were obliged to operate from bases in Japan. Disguised North Korean guerrillas mingling with the hordes of refugees hindered American progress still further. Despite round-the-clock bombing of North Korean troop columns, bridges, and marshalling yards by American and Australian planes, piloted by European war veterans, the advance continued. The first American tanks landed in Korea on 7 July but by this time the Americans and South Koreans, greatly outnumbered, had retreated to the Kum river to defend Taejon.

On 18 July the U.S. 1st Cavalry Division, veteran troops of the Pacific war, landed with more tanks and artillery at Pohang. The North Koreans, however, conscious that success depended upon a quick victory before America and the United Nations could successfully intervene, pressed relentlessly southwards. The Kum river line collapsed as tanks forded the river on 15 July and on 21 July Taejon, already ablaze, was evacuated.

By the close of July large parts of the American 8th Army, distinguished at the Normandy landings, had arrived in Korea with armour. The Second Infantry Division landed at Pusan on 31 July after crossing the Pacific in only 10 days. It was followed 24 hours later by the 1st Marine Division which had fought at Guadalcanal and was accompanied by flame-throwers, bazookas, and 45-ton 'Pershing' tanks. As they arrived they were thrown piecemeal into the conflict in a holding operation to gain time to construct a secure base. Despite the presence of these veteran troops the American bridgehead at Pusan was in grave danger of being overrun. On 3 August, following the fall of Chinju, 60 miles west of Pusan, almost all the American and South Korean forces withdrew across the Naktong river, blew its bridges, and took up positions in the hills beyond. Enclosed in a small 'defence box' the Americans seemed likely to be driven into the sea (see Map 6a).

41 August 1950. A North Korean factory near Kwanju in flames after direct hits from American fighters and divebombers

42 Refugees in the evacuation of Taejon

The port of Pohang, which had the best airfield in the defence perimeter, was captured on 11 August although American Negro troops clung on to the air-strip under fire. Co-ordination between American ground forces was made more difficult by the mountainous terrain and Negro troops in the hills overlooking Chinju were forced to evacuate after being bombarded by their own artillery. Inside the defence box the activities of North Korean guerrillas made the situation even more dangerous. On 17 August in response to a call from their commander, General Kim Ir. Sen, for 'victory before the end of August' the North Koreans launched an offensive across the Naktong. This was temporarily halted the following day after heavy North Korean losses and the pressure was somewhat eased by the South Korean recapture of Pohang. The onslaught resumed on 1 September with the heaviest North Korean attack since the beginning of the war along a 50-mile front from Changnyong to the south coast. Under cover of darkness the Naktong river was crossed in 17 places, causeways of logs and sandbags being used to carry the tanks. By 2 September the entire U.N. air force had been flung into the battle in support of the ground forces. 440 sorties were flown by mid-afternoon on that day and again the offensive was held.

The situation was, however, still critical. General Douglas MacArthur, American Commander-in-Chief Far East, hero of the Pacific war, and virtually viceroy of post-war Japan, had been made commander of the U.N. forces in Korea on 7 July. By the close of July 50 nations had pledged assistance to the U.N. in their police action in Korea. By early September, however, only a self-contained British force which landed from Hongkong on 29 August, had been sent to reinforce the Americans who had borne the burden of the ground fighting and already suffered 8,000 casualties. The British government had realised that if the Western allies did not support America over Korea NATO had little hope of survival. Urgent pleas now went out to other U.N. members to reinforce the Korea front without delay. Eventually contingents were sent from 14 other nations but by this time the war had been completely transformed by a daring gamble of General MacArthur.

At dawn on 15 September the 10th U.S. Army Corps and part of the 1st Marine Division carried out an amphibious landing at the west-coast port of Inchon, 150 miles behind North Korean lines and only 20 miles from Seoul. Simultaneously South Korean forces landed on the east coast again behind North Korean lines at Yongdok, north of Pohang (see Map 6a). The Inchon landing was a desperate venture. The port was approached through a narrow channel studded with shoals; the tides would only carry vessels into the harbour for about three hours. There were no beaches and the marines would be forced to scale from their landing craft a 12-foot sea wall. To provide troops for the assault would gravely weaken the forces around Pusan. Despite all criticisms MacArthur was adamant. The area around Inchon and Seoul was the vital bottleneck in North Korean communications with the front around Pusan. If this could be cut the North Korean forces in the south would be left isolated and the war brought to a dramatic end.

Watched by MacArthur the impossible landing at Inchon was an outstanding success. The North Koreans were taken completely by surprise. Kimpo airfield fell on 17 September and three days later American marines crossed the Han river in amphibious tractors and cut the road between Seoul and Pyongyang. At the same time U.N. forces broke out of the Pusan defence box and began to press north, parallel with the South Korean forces advancing up the east coast (see Map 6a).

By 21 September the marines from Inchon had reached Seoul. Here they met

43 The American contingent of the U.N. forces at Inchon

desperate resistance. 20,000 defenders had built stone barricades and dug trenches in the streets. As the marines entered the city it became a blazing inferno:

> They ground slowly forward under a hail of protecting artillery, mortar fire and close air support which levelled whole acres. The defenders fought with great tenacity to the end firing from roof tops, trees, and side streets. Intense heat from the burning buildings added to the nightmare . . . suicide squads attacked American tanks.[1]

Finally the 90 mm. guns of the tanks blasted down the barricades and 'surrounded by hills blazing with napalm and huge smiling posters of Stalin and Kim Il Sung, the stars and stripes at last floated over the shattered fifth city of Asia'.[2] Seoul had paid dearly for its liberation. In addition to the 20,000 Communist defenders, 30,000 civilians were also dead – killed by the results of the massive American fire-power and the close-support tactics developed in World War II. A further 20,000 civilians, suspected of right-wing sympathies, had been executed before the Americans arrived and many others deported to concentration camps in North Korea. MacArthur's 'one great blow', however, appeared to have brought the war to an end. As U.N. forces pursued the broken remnants of the Korean People's Army towards the 38th parallel, the U.N. forces from Seoul made contact with those advancing from the south-east. The North Korean army, which had lost 335,000 men, had ceased to exist. Great numerical superiority had been effectively countered by the superiority in weapons, fire-power, and training of the U.N. Having successfully repelled the aggressors, the U.N. had now to decide whether they should call a halt or cross the 38th parallel and unify the two parts of Korea under a freely elected government. Politically this policy was wise, but it was militarily dangerous since it would bring American troops to the Chinese borders and by the elimination of one of their satellites present a direct challenge to the Communist bloc.

For Syngman Rhee, who had returned to Seoul on 29 September expressing 'the undying gratitude of the Korean people' to the American and U.N. forces, the course was obvious. 'The 38th parallel', he declared 'no longer exists . . . we will go on to the natural northern boundaries of our country.' Ernest Bevin, the British Foreign

[1] D. Rees, *Korea: the Limited War* (Macmillan), pp. 91–2.   [2] D. Rees, op. cit., p. 92.

44 American marines march captured
North Koreans from a cornfield bordering
Kimpo airfield

45 September 1950. An American
soldier patrols the streets of Inchon
after its capture from the North Koreans

Secretary, and General MacArthur also thought that the time had come to unify Korea. On 7 October the General Assembly of the U.N. adopted a vaguely worded British resolution authorising the U.N. forces to take all appropriate steps 'to ensure conditions of stability in Korea'. The Americans, however, had already decided to cross the parallel. Despite warnings of Chinese intervention they believed that neither the Chinese nor the Russians would be prepared to fight. When the North Korean government ignored an ultimatum for unconditional surrender MacArthur's U.N. forces crossed into North Korea on 1 October.

Strengthened by the arrival of Australian and Turkish contingents they struck rapidly towards the Yalu river. North Korean resistance was slight. Pyongyang, 'the first Iron Curtain capital,' was taken on 19 October, and South Korean police began mass executions of Communist sympathisers until stopped in disgust by British and U.N. troops. In the last days of October, however, resistance grew stiffer and the presence of Chinese troops was reported among North Korean forces. On 27 October a Chinese force crossed the Yalu to protect the Suito dam on the Manchurian bank of the river, which provided electricity for Manchurian and North Korean industry. On 4 November Peking Radio announced that people throughout China were volunteering to help North Korea to resist American aggression. In the north-east the South Koreans suddenly found themselves in danger of encirclement by a strong force of 10,000, including Chinese. In the north-west British, American, and South Korean forces were forced to retreat by counter-attacks supported by tanks. On 8 November 80 Super-fortresses escorted by 200 fighters destroyed the Sinuiju bridges over the Yalu, but it was too late. Since 16 October some 500,000 Chinese had crossed the frontier into North Korea, and the U.N. was confronted by a large, fresh army with a reserve and supplies beyond the reach of its planes in Manchuria.

On 24 November as the weather deteriorated and snow fell MacArthur launched his final offensive to reach the Yalu. 'If successful', he stated, 'this should end the war.' The 'boys' would be able to eat their Christmas dinner at home. For many, however, the Thanksgiving Day turkey dinner supplied by air on 23 November was to be their last meal. The size of the Chinese army which had crossed into Korea had not been realised. Travelling by night and hiding by day it had escaped observation from the air. MacArthur's hopes were shattered when on 25 November the U.N. advance was flung back by a violent counter-attack (see Map 6b). A wedge was driven into the U.N. lines

58

46 American forces on the road to
Seoul after the capture of Inchon

47 American artillery in action. The
Chinese were forced back by violent
'meat grinder' tactics

at Tokchon, and as the Chinese wheeled westwards to trap the U.N. forces MacArthur
realised that he was facing not 'People's Volunteers' but 'major sections of the Chinese
Continental army'. By 27 November the U.N. battalions were retreating over the
Chongchon river and southwards towards Pyongyang, while in the north-east the South
Koreans were driven back by 80,000 Chinese supported by tanks. The American 2nd
Division retreating down the Kunuri-Sunchon road found a Chinese division dug in on
both sides of the route for 6 miles.

> The leading vehicles were soon picked off jamming the road as the intensity of the
> enemy fire increased. . . . There were between thirty and forty machine guns and ten
> mortars firing onto the road. There was no place to hide as the storm of steel beat down
> on the Americans for the knocked-out trucks, jeeps, tanks, and weapon carriers . . .
> offered no protection to the demoralised, tottering infantry. . . . Napalm trickled down
> the hillside from the furious air strikes which had . . . failed to stop the division's
> agony. . . .[1]

As victory turned to defeat MacArthur announced that 'we face an entirely new
war . . . a state of undeclared war exists between Communist China and the U.N.
forces'. As the retreat continued he began to press for direct action against Chinese
territory by sea and air. U.N. command of the air was limited by the fact that he could
not bomb Chinese bases north of the Yalu, and it began to be rumoured that he had
requested permission to use the atomic bomb. The Cold War in Asia had suddenly
become a hot war in which all the major powers were involved to some degree and
which threatened to erupt into World War III.

By 5 December the U.N. had blown up its installations and retreated from
Pyongyang beyond the 38th parallel to cover Seoul. In the north-east, following the
evacuation of Wonsan on 7 December, U.N. forces retreated through mountainous
country, and snow-storms which deprived them of air support, to the port of Hungnam.
Throughout their retreat they were ambushed and harried by the Chinese who were
now estimated to have two of their five field armies in Korea commanded by Lin Piao.
Between 13 and 24 December 105,000 U.N. troops plus their equipment and supplies
were evacuated by sea from Hungnam together with 100,000 refugees. North Korea was
lost to the U.N. The victory at Inchon was cancelled out and China, the first Communist

[1] D. Rees, op. cit., p. 159.

state to defeat a Western army in a major battle, had emerged overnight as a world power.

On 24 December Lt.-Gen. Matthew Ridgway, who had commanded the U.S. Airborne Division in Italy, Normandy, the Ardennes, and Germany, had taken command of the ground forces in Korea on the death of Lt.-Gen. Walton Walker. He did not arrive a moment too soon. Defeatism was spreading and the soldiers, hourly expecting another offensive, did not know why they were fighting. Chinese tactics and the intense cold, which reduced many men to tears, were particularly responsible for the alarming decline in morale. The Chinese attacked in waves regardless of casualties. Their attacks were frequently at night and were accompanied by terrifying noises from trumpets, drums, rattles, and shepherds' pipes.

Ridgway did not have long to restore the spirit of his shattered troops. At dawn on 1 January 1951 the Chinese, reinforced from Manchuria, launched a New Year offensive designed to complete the conquest of Korea. Crossing the frozen Imjin river massed forces of infantry advanced through the barbed wire and minefields screaming 'Kill G.I.'. In two days the U.N. navy and air force flew 1,500 sorties in an attempt to stem the tide but despite heavy losses the Chinese drove a two-mile wedge into U.N. lines. On 3 January Seoul, abandoned by four-fifths of its population, changed hands for the third time. Kimpo airport was demolished, the ice on the Han river was mortared, and its bridges blown as the U.N. retreated. Other U.N. troops and 10,000 refugees were evacuated from Inchon under cover of naval gunfire. After three days' heavy fighting in blinding snow-storms the U.N. evacuated the rail junction of Wonju but by this time the impetus of the Chinese attack was losing power. The Chinese soldier went into battle carrying only sufficient food for six days. When this was gone he had to withdraw temporarily from the line. It had also become obvious that the Chinese, ill-equipped, lightly-armed, and with poor field communications, relied mainly upon sheer weight of numbers for success.

The policy of subduing North Korea was now abandoned by the U.N. who in the light of Chinese weaknesses began a grim war of containment. The object of this war was slowly and systematically to force the Chinese back to the 38th parallel hill by hill, and by killing as many of their soldiers as possible eventually to force them to negotiate a peace. The new tactics became known to the troops as the 'meat grinder'.

> You began with the long range artillery . . . enveloping the hills in tall columns of dust flung up by tons of high explosive, followed by the quicker shell bursts from the more accurate lighter guns at a shorter range. You bombarded the positions further with tank guns whilst swooping aircraft plastered them with napalm and rockets and the infantrymen secure in their foxholes let loose a murderous hail of staccato fire with rifles, machine guns, and mortars. This lasted for the morning. In the afternoon the infantry crept up the slopes of the hills to find out if anyone was left. . . .[1]

As the Chinese advance slackened Wonju with its air-strip was retaken on 22 January and the limited U.N. advance began. By the end of the month U.N. forces now reinforced by Turkish, French, and Greek troops held a continual coast-to-coast line a hundred miles long. Bitter hand-to-hand fighting with bayonets and grenades developed as they met the main Chinese defences protecting Seoul. 8,000 gallons of napalm were dropped in one day to burn the Chinese from their foxholes in the ghastly

[1] R. O. Holles, *Now Thrive the Armourers* (Harrap), pp. 76–7.

horror of modern warfare. Hill 431, north-west of Suwon, changed hands five times in 24 hours as the fighting swung to and fro. On 5 February the U.N. landed five armoured columns, the biggest tank concentration of the war, in an all-out effort to recapture Seoul. The Chinese rushed tanks on plank bridges over the Han river and fought so desperately at close quarters that many were crushed under the treads of U.N. tanks. By the close of the day they had suffered 2,000 casualties but the U.N. had reached the outskirts of Seoul. A Chinese counter-attack in the central sector of the front on 12 February was halted within 10 miles of Wonju. 5,000 more Chinese were killed in one day. By 9 March as the melting snows and torrential rains turned the terrain to a sea of mud the U.N. crossed the Han river and occupied Seoul for the fourth time. After a further 19,000 casualties in two days the Chinese were reported to be withdrawing on all fronts, and on 3 April the U.N. crossed the 38th parallel once more.

48   20 April 1951. General MacArthur is welcomed by Cardinal Spellman, Archbishop of New York

Attention from this triumph was, however, diverted by a political storm which suddenly burst in America centred around General MacArthur, the U.N. commander-in-chief. MacArthur believed that by their actions the Chinese had begun a Third World War. His solution was decisively to crush communism in Asia before Russia had gained equality with America in atomic weapons whatever the risk. In this view he was supported by influential members of the Republican Party still smarting under the Communist victory in China, and a large section of the American public. While the American and British governments and the United Nations were anxious to keep the Korean war a 'limited war' which would not spread, MacArthur wished 'to inflict such a destructive blow upon Red China's capacity to wage aggressive war that it would remove her as a further threat to peace in Asia for generations to come'. To this end he proposed a coastal blockade of China to prevent her obtaining war supplies; the destruction of China's flimsy industry by naval and air attack; and the use of Chiang's Nationalist troops from Formosa to reinforce the U.N. in Korea and invade the Chinese mainland. There was a strong feeling, too, that he wished to use the atomic bomb. Nor did MacArthur try to conceal his differences with the Truman government and his bitterness at the restrictions placed upon his actions. Instead they were made public in a series of statements which eventually on 11 April led to his recall by Truman for insubordination. Relieved of all his commands he returned to America on 17 April. A crowd of 500,000 people acclaimed him as he landed at San Francisco and on 19 April in New York he was cheered hysterically by $7\frac{1}{2}$ million citizens, the greatest crowd that had ever gathered in the city.

> The figure of the general standing up in the back of his car dressed in trench coat and battered cap was often invisible because of the blizzard of paper which poured down from the skyscrapers. As he passed men and women crossed themselves. When the motorcade approached . . . the City Hall the shouts rose to hysteria. . . . There he is. . . . There he is. . . .[1]

In an address to Congress MacArthur condemned the appeasement of Red China and it seemed as if the Truman government might be swept away in the political storm which followed. While the debate raged, Ridgway, MacArthur's successor, was confronted with a massive Chinese spring counter-offensive which carried the Chinese again across the 38th parallel. Wave after wave of suicide attacks made the mass slaughter of Chinese the bloodiest in modern times. In the minefields 55-gallon drums of napalm and petrol were detonated by electricity. 12,000 were slain on the first day of the offensive and by 26 May the U.N. had driven them back to the parallel and crossed into North Korea. By 22 June the U.N. had destroyed the 'Iron Triangle' of Pyonggang, Chorwon, and Kumha, the base from which the Communists had launched their spring offensive. Here the U.N. halted (see Map 6b). In America the success of Ridgway's 'holding war' began to win back support for Truman. In Korea the failure of the spring counter-offensive had proved that a modern army of moderate size with heavy fire-power could smash head-on the mass attacks of poorly equipped infantry despite their courage and fanaticism. Total Communist casualties in the first year of the war were estimated at over a million. The dream of easy conquest by weight of numbers was gone. The U.N. held a continuous line across Korea which the Communists could neither break nor outflank. The war had become a stalemate. On 23 June 1951 proposals for a settlement through the negotiation of a cease-fire followed by an armistice and a withdrawal of troops were made by M. Malik, the Soviet representative at the United Nations. On 30 June a broadcast offer was made by General Ridgway of a meeting to discuss an armistice, which was accepted on 1 July by China and North Korea.

Those who expected a speedy end to the war were disappointed. The negotiations continued for over two years before the cease-fire was finally signed. Once the truce negotiations began U.N. military operations were curtailed so that there was little incentive for the Communists to make peace. Instead they skilfully used the negotiations to launch a world-wide propaganda campaign and to construct a defensive network across Korea much more massive than any trench system of World War I and designed to resist even atomic attack. The acquisition of large numbers of Russian aircraft also rapidly transformed China into one of the world's major air powers. Since two static defence systems now confronted each other the remainder of the military operations

---

[1] D. Rees, op. cit., p. 227.

consisted largely of skirmishing for vital hills and outposts. Nevertheless, during these two years the U.N. lost a further 60,000 men.

The first cease-fire negotiations, which began at Kaesong on 10 July 1951, lasted only until 23 August when they were broken off since the Communists insisted upon a U.N. withdrawal to the indefensible 38th parallel. They were resumed once more at Panmunjon on 25 October only to reach deadlock over the repatriation of prisoners-of-war. While the Communists insisted upon compulsory repatriation of all prisoners-of-war, since many anti-Communists did not wish to return, the U.N. wanted repatriation upon a voluntary basis. When prisoner-of-war lists were examined it seemed that a large number of American soldiers and South Korean soldiers and civilians had died after capture by the Communists. The Chinese accused the Americans of germ warfare and the Americans countered with accusations of the 'brainwashing' of prisoners. While the bitter wrangling continued Syngman Rhee, who had consistently tried to prevent an armistice, in May 1952 declared martial law in South Korea, arrested twelve members of the National Assembly, and attempted to make himself a dictator.

In an attempt to break the deadlock the U.N. launched a series of massive air strikes against North Korea. The Japanese-built Suito power station, which was the fourth largest in the world and supplied North Korea and Manchuria with much of their electricity, was destroyed on 23 June 1952. On 11 July, 1,200 planes dropped 1,400 tons of bombs and 23,000 gallons of napalm on Pyongyang. A similar raid took place on 29 August but had no effect upon the Chinese and North Koreans.

In November 1952 the Republican, General Eisenhower, won the American presidential election upon a pledge to end the Korean war. The American public hoped that the veteran campaigner of World War II might find a successful solution but after a personal visit to Korea in December he also returned baffled by the military stalemate. In these circumstances Eisenhower and his new Secretary of State, John Foster Dulles, began to reconsider MacArthur's policy of a direct attack upon China. The risks were great and British disapproval was as strong as it had been towards MacArthur's views. Nevertheless, it was hinted in January 1953 that unless a truce was forthcoming

49   Panmunjon. U.N. tanks on guard near the North and South Korean dividing line – a situation which has lasted since the 1953 armistice

Formosa might be used to launch operations against the Chinese mainland. The strain upon China's economy was undoubtedly growing greater with over a million troops confronting the 768,000 of the U.N. force in Korea. Two other factors finally decided the Chinese to end the Korean war. On 5 March 1953 Stalin died. The following night each Chinese soldier along the front fired a last salute to the Russian leader. His departure, however, brought with it the threat of a disputed succession, and in these circumstances Russia would not be anxious for a direct confrontation with America.

The second factor was the threat of atomic war against mainland China. In May nuclear weapons were despatched without too much secrecy to Okinawa and Dulles informed Indian officials that the war would be extended to China unless a Korean armistice was signed. This information was duly passed on to Peking. On 27 July 1953 despite a last-minute attempt by Syngman Rhee to disrupt the proceedings the 'talking war' came to an end and the armistice was signed. There was no compulsory repatriation of prisoners. The dividing line between North and South Korea remained roughly the same as when the war began. Four of the five great powers had been involved in armed conflict but the war had not spread, perhaps because none were ready for total war so soon after 1945, or perhaps because none thought Korea worth fighting for. America, which had borne the brunt of the fighting, had successfully contained communism and had also vindicated the authority of the United Nations. Her success had cost her 142,000 American, 300,000 South Korean, and 17,000 non-Korean casualties. Many Americans regretted that they had not forced the issue with world communism when nuclear superiority was theirs.

China at the expense of $1\frac{1}{2}$ million Chinese and half a million North Korean dead had established a buffer state on her eastern frontier. Formosa and the offshore islands of Quemoy-Matsu, which she would inevitably have captured in 1950–1, however, passed under the protection of the American 7th Fleet. Russia, who by the close of 1950 had 5,000 technicians, engineers, and pilots in North Korea and Manchuria, had without cost strengthened for the time being her connections with China, which was obliged to look to her for supplies of military equipment. Syngman Rhee on 8 August secured American protection for South Korea by a mutual security treaty. His corrupt régime was overthrown in April 1960, but even when South Korea became a military dictatorship in May 1961 American guided nuclear missiles still remained to guard all invasion routes from the North.

The greatest losers were the Koreans themselves. 'The land of the morning calm' was left a desert in which 3 million Korean civilians had perished through the ravages of a modern war whose effects could hardly have been worse if the atomic bomb had been used. No peace treaty was signed, and the final battle line remained a fortified frontier between two states which had no diplomatic relations with each other. Technically the war has never ended and each month the Military Armistice Committee still meets at Panmunjon to enable Communist and U.N. representatives to slang each other for breaches of the armistice. Elsewhere in Asia, however, it proved less easy to contain Chinese communism, which believed Asia had to be unified for world revolution.

7 Communist Revolution in South-East Asia

AS THE COMMUNISTS completed the conquest of China and war raged in Korea, the whole of South-East Asia grew into a major theatre of the Cold War. Until December 1941 all of South-East Asia, except Thailand, containing almost a quarter of the world's population had been controlled by the Western colonial powers. There had been little sign of any movement for national independence until the victorious Japanese armies swept across the area proving that the Europeans were not invincible. In many places the Japanese had first encouraged native and nationalist movements since these were hostile to the Western powers. Later, as Japanese rule grew more oppressive, anti-Japanese guerrilla resistance movements appeared in which the Communists, as in Europe, played the leading part. Western Imperial rule had in most countries brought few benefits. Poverty was intense and support for the Communists grew as they identified themselves with the nationalists. In the last stages of the Pacific war, British and American forces allied with local nationalists and Communists to drive out the Japanese. Many of the weapons supplied to the guerrillas were, however, buried for future use against the returning colonial authorities. In the face of demands for national independence it was obvious in 1945 that there could be no return to the pre-war position in South-East Asia. The Western colonial powers, however, followed no common policy. America, having crushed an attempt by the Communist resistance movement, the Huks, to set up a 'People's democratic government', granted independence to the Philippines in 1946 although keeping military bases in the islands. Great extremes of wealth and poverty, harsh absentee landlords, and corrupt government, however, did much to keep communism alive.

Britain, like America undefeated in World War II, was also able to make

50 Dien Bien Phu, March 1954. Pieces of a French
transport plane, shot down by the Viet Minh, land before
a French Legionnaire

65

concessions from a position of strength. She was doubtless also influenced by her impending bankruptcy. India, Pakistan, Burma, and Ceylon, were released in 1947 although the British did not withdraw from Singapore, Hongkong, or Malaya. The two former colonies were regarded as vital naval bases for the protection of British Far Eastern interests. Malayan independence was given little consideration. There was no strong nationalist movement among its mixed population, while its rubber was a vital export for British post-war reconstruction.

The Dutch and the French, both defeated in the war, were not so fortunate. When they refused to grant independence to their former colonies, the Dutch East Indies and French Indo-China, nationalist rebellions mushroomed into full-scale wars.

In the Dutch East Indies nationalist uprisings in Java and Sumatra in 1945 were aided by the retreating Japanese who allowed large quantities of arms to pass into Indonesian hands. On 17 August 1945, two days after Japan's surrender and before British troops had arrived, Achmet Sukarno, the nationalist leader and a Japanese collaborator, proclaimed the republic of Indonesia at Djakarta. The Dutch, however, refused to recognise the new republic and from November 1946 to December 1949 Dutch armies fought a bitter battle with the nationalists. The war was virtually won by the Dutch when in December 1948 Sukarno and the other Indonesian leaders were captured after a brilliant paratroop action at Jogjakarta. They were, however, compelled to withdraw by the United Nations where both America and India were highly critical of the Dutch action, and in December 1949 Sukarno's Indonesia finally secured its full independence. America hoped by this policy to gain the support of the new Indonesia against Communist China. Holland was a small country with a large empire which was obliged to bow to international opinion. France, with the right of veto in the U.N. Security Council, was in a much stronger position to defy world opinion in Indo-China, which consisted of Vietnam, Cambodia, and Laos (see Map 11). France was not only determined to profit from her large pre-war investments in Vietnam's rice-growing industry but also was anxious to rebuild her international power and prestige which had been badly damaged by her collapse in 1940 and her subsequent evacuation of

52 Vo Nguyen Giap,
later Defence Minister
of North Vietnam

Syria. In Vietnam the war-time nationalist movement was not only anti-Japanese but also anti-French and Communist led. Its leader, Ho Chi Minh, had been a Comintern agent in Vietnam since 1925. As early as 1930 he had formed the Communist Party of Indo-China, thus showing his intention of freeing not only Vietnam but also Laos and Cambodia from French Imperial rule. Jailed by the British in Hongkong in the early thirties, Ho reappeared in Vietnam in 1941 to found his resistance movement for Vietnamese Communists and nationalists – the Viet Minh. The Viet Minh received arms from the Allies which again were later used against the French.

As the Japanese war ended the land was occupied by British troops to the south and Chinese Nationalist troops to the north of the 16th parallel. When French forces eventually arrived in October 1945 they were able to reassert their authority in the south but not in the north where at Hanoi Ho had declared the independence of all Vietnam and established a government claiming authority over it. Bao Dai, the Vietnamese emperor who had collaborated with Japan, resigned, but the French had no such ideas. When negotiations with Ho broke down they began to prepare for the reconquest of Vietnam from the south northward. In December 1946 the Viet Minh commander, Vo Nguyen Giap, a former history teacher whose wife had died in a French prison, launched an offensive against the French forces in Tongking. Giap, who was violently anti-French, had received a training in guerrilla warfare, for which he had a particular aptitude, with the Chinese Communists at Yenan. He had had ample opportunity to practise Mao Tse-Tung's theories of revolutionary war against the Japanese.

By 1946 he commanded at least 10,000 men. The first Indo-China war, which was to last eight years, had begun. By 1948, as tension mounted in Europe with Communist successes in Greece and the approach of the Berlin blockade, Giap had shown that his guerrilla army was able to keep the French at bay. In China the Communists had begun their victorious drive southwards, and as world communism seemed successful everywhere, Communist risings broke out almost simultaneously in the Philippines, Burma, Indonesia, and Malaya.

67

In September 1947 a meeting of the Cominform in Poland had announced that the time was ripe for colonial peoples 'to expel their oppressors'. More detailed instructions for rebellion were issued at a Communist-sponsored Asian Youth Conference held in Calcutta in February 1948, after which the delegates returned home to prepare for revolution. None of the uprisings succeeded. In Burma, where the Communists had previously accepted the plan for independence, they suddenly denounced it and resorted to arms but with little effect. Burma was already independent when the rising began. National feeling was satisfied and communism won little support. The Philippines, too, were independent, but here the Communists enjoyed some early success. Freedom had failed to improve the miserable lot of the peasantry and the Communists

53   February 1949. Lt.-Gen. Suharto (later President; *right*) receives instructions near Jogjakarta from Panglima Besar Soedirman (*left*) the Indonesian supreme commander in the war against the Dutch

54   President Sukarno visits the new Indonesian University with his second wife, Fatmawati

appealed to them rather than to national feeling. The Huks, officially disbanded in 1945, had already dug up their arms again in face of oppression by the government and landlords, and taken to the hills. By mid-1950 they controlled a number of rural areas and provincial capitals. Within three years, however, their army was broken and in September 1954 its leader, Luis Taruc, surrendered. The Communist defeat was largely the work of Ramon Magsaysay who became Minister of Defence in September 1950 when Huk success seemed imminent. A month after his appointment the Philippine army captured over one hundred Communist leaders and thus broke the basis of Huk organisation. Magsaysay, backed by American advisers, combined force with friendship. Huks who surrendered were given money and land. Corruption was eliminated in the government and the army; peasants were protected from the oppression of landlords. When Magsaysay swept to victory as the Philippine President in 1953 he had won over many of his former enemies, who had never been convinced Communists, by removing the grievances which had driven them to support the Huks.

In Indonesia, the largest and most important of the South-East Asian countries, with its 3,000 islands, the Communist revolution again enjoyed short shrift. By 1948 the Indonesian Communist Party was large in size and also controlled the trade unions. It had, however, no war-time resistance army upon which to build, since Sukarno and the nationalists had collaborated with the Japanese. When the call to rebellion came the Communist forces were ill-prepared and easily crushed. The Communist base at Madiun in Java was captured by Sukarno's nationalists in October. Musso, the Moscow-trained Communist leader, died in battle and the remaining leaders were shot. At this time the Indonesians were still fighting the Dutch. Sukarno and his nationalists were regarded as the real heroes of independence and not surprisingly the Communists secured little support. Later, however, they were to try again.

In Malaya where in 1948 the question of independence was not envisaged by the British, the Communist insurrection at first came close to success. Communism had established itself in Malaya in the late twenties among the large Chinese population, imported to work in the tin-mines and rubber plantations, which had few civic or political rights. It made little impression upon the native Malays and Indians who were relatively contented with their lot. Suppressed by the British police throughout the thirties the Malayan Communist Party offered its services to the British as a resistance movement when the Japanese invaded. The offer was reluctantly accepted and by early 1942 the Malayan Communist Party had developed into the Malayan People's Anti-Japanese Army (MPAJA). Driven into the jungle by the Japanese the MPAJA grew in strength, recruiting principally among the Chinese squatters who lived on the jungle edges. From 1944 it received considerable supplies of British arms. When the war ended in August 1945 it emerged from the jungle to disarm the Japanese and take control. With few British troops in Malaya and the Malayan Chinese population intensely proud of its Chinese guerrilla army, a Communist takeover was feasible. The Communists, however, held back, fearing perhaps that Chinese Nationalist troops might be sent temporarily to occupy Malaya as they had done French Indo-China. Gradually the British re-established control. Some of the British and Japanese weapons were surrendered but others were kept for future use. Some 4,000 of the best guerrillas in the MPAJA remained in hiding. The remaining 6,000 were disbanded but stayed on call ready for the final uprising to drive the British from Malaya. To this end Communist cells were also planted in the trade unions.

As the British prepared to evacuate Burma many Communists thought that force might be unnecessary and Malaya would be next. When these hopes were dashed, encouraged by Communist success in Greece, French Indo-China, and particularly China, a series of strikes in 1947 paved the way for the Malayan uprising. Contact between the Malayan and Chinese Communist parties had always been quite close, and Chen Ping, who had been one of the Malayan contingent in the London VJ Day celebrations, had also visited Communist China in 1945 and 1946. He returned duly impressed with the success of Mao Tse-Tung's methods of guerrilla warfare which the Malayan Communists proceeded to adopt. Lau Yew, who was given military control of the rising, began to form in February 1948 the Malayan People's Anti-British Army (MPABA). Recruitment was largely from the disbanded members of the MPAJA. Special 'terror units' encouraged volunteers and reluctant reservists to make for the jungle camps where the hidden arms were recovered and distributed.

Chen Ping planned to establish a Communist Malayan republic in accordance with the three stages which had won Mao Tse-Tung control of China. During stage one guerrilla warfare was to drive the Europeans, police, and government officials from the small towns and villages, the tin-mines and rubber plantations. Guerrilla bases could then be established in these 'liberated areas' where the insurgent army could assemble, train, and gather strength before it finally crushed the British forces in the larger towns in conventional battle. Optimists hoped for practical assistance from Russia or China and considered that the British might withdraw before the final stage rather than become involved in a struggle similar to that in Palestine which they were just leaving.

The Communist campaign commenced in April and May 1948. Acts of violence, including the murder of Chinese Nationalists, Europeans, and Malays, were accompanied by strikes in tin-mines, rubber plantations, and other industries. On 13 June with 5,000 workers involved in 23 strikes, the Communist-dominated Pan-Malayan Federation of Trade Unions was declared illegal by the British High Commissioner, who three days later proclaimed a state of emergency as the result of the murder by Chinese terrorists of three British planters in Perak. A general Communist 'call to arms' followed which heralded the beginning of a 12-year guerrilla war. The British were undoubtedly unprepared for the size and violence of the Communist attack. As the police received additional powers of search, detention, and curfew, the armed forces were brought in to help. Planters and estate workers were formed into local constabularies and Sten-guns issued to defend plantations against terrorist attack. Several hundred ex-Palestine policemen were rushed to Malaya to train hastily enrolled special constables, while the R.A.F. began to bomb terrorist camps. These steps encouraged Europeans to remain on isolated estates, thus frustrating the first stage of the Communist plan. A radio network kept contact with even the remotest police posts in the towns and villages to enable them to send for aid.

When terrorist attacks failed to produce the mass evacuation expected Lau Yew ordered attacks in greater strength to overwhelm the defenders of police stations and mines. On 27 June 40 gunmen attacked a police station at Kuala Krau with tommy-guns, killing the wife of a Malay policeman before being driven off. Two days later other terrorists burned a police station and looted shops at Jerantut. The coal-mining centre of Batu Arang was seized and held for a time on 12 July by a hundred Communists who killed five Chinese and destroyed the mining machinery. Such attacks inevitably brought losses, and on 16 July Lau Yew and ten other terrorists were killed in a jungle clash with police near Kapang. His death almost brought about the collapse of the terrorist forces. No liberated areas had been gained, morale was low, and many city Communists had yet to learn to live in the jungle. Ferret force teams of British, Malay, and Gurkha soldiers, specially trained in jungle warfare and using Dyak head-hunters as trackers, were working in the jungles locating and directing security forces to the guerrilla camps. The Communists were saved only by a sudden pause in government activity caused by the accidental death in an air crash on 2 July of the High Commissioner, Sir Edward Gent. There was a long delay in appointing a successor; the Ferret forces were withdrawn, reinforcements were held up, and the initiative passed to the Communists, who in February 1949 renamed their army the Malayan Races' Liberation Army.

This attempt to attract Malays and Indians enjoyed little success. The 5,000 guerrillas remained largely Chinese dependent upon the Min Yuen, an underground organisation in the Chinese squatter villages, which provided food, money, and communications. Their movements were hampered by a strict system of identity cards and the deportation of large numbers of Chinese sympathisers from the villages to dreaded Nationalist China. By the time Lt.-Gen. Sir Harold Briggs was made Director of Operations in Malaya in April 1950 the Communists had been obliged to revert by difficulties and heavy losses to terrorism and guerrilla war. Briggs, who had fought in Burma, had much experience of jungle warfare. In June 1950 he introduced the 'Briggs Plan' which began the clearance of terrorists from Malaya by separating them from their village supporters, thus driving them into the open. To this end Briggs began resettling the squatter villages in 'Resettlement Areas' out of Communist reach and protected by barbed wire and special constables. By February 1952 over 400,000 squatters had been moved into 400 'New Villages'. The Ferret forces were also revived and strict food controls introduced. Cafés were closed; shops recorded all food sold; and workers were not allowed to take food to work. As 'Operation Starvation' tightened, Communist policy changed. Initially much terrorism and blackmail had been used to secure the support of villagers. This now ceased as the Communists realised the need to gain the voluntary support of the masses.

The British suffered yet another setback, however, when on 6 October the new High Commissioner, Sir Henry Gurney, was ambushed and killed north of Kuala

55 Communist suspects are rounded up by British troops and Malay special police

56 High Commissioner Sir Gerald Templer (*facing camera*) talks to British officers

Lumpur by 38 terrorists. A month later ill-health forced Briggs to resign. The offices of High Commissioner and Director of Operations were, however, combined in February 1952 in the person of General Sir Gerald Templer. Templer not only raised hope and morale by vigorously continuing the drive against the Communists but also brought with him a plan for hastening Malayan independence. This won the support of the Malays who hitherto had been disinterested in the struggle. Parallel with this political action Templer also determinedly continued the Briggs Plan. Resettlement and food regulations were vigorously enforced. Secret questionnaires were used in towns and villages to secure information about Communists and large rewards were offered for their death or capture. The latter were often criticised since they were greater than a constable could hope to earn in a lifetime. When villages were discovered to have collaborated with guerrillas collective punishment was inflicted.

71

During 1952 security forces killed 1,097 guerrillas, often as a result of information given – a good indication that Templer was winning the battle for 'the hearts and minds' of the people. While 'voice aircraft', equipped with loudspeakers, dropped leaflets and safe-conduct passes and urged Communists to surrender, hunter-killer platoons continued their grim work in the jungle. Planes were also used for spraying the guerrillas' jungle gardens with plant-killing chemicals to deprive them of crops. Short of food and harassed by security forces the Communists were driven still deeper into the jungle. Occasional supplies, arms, and advisers arrived from Communist China, but since China was heavily committed in Korea and elsewhere there was none of the large-scale help anticipated. By the time Templer left Malaya in May 1954 restrictions had been lifted from a number of areas which had been cleared of Communists and declared 'white'. By the time Malayan independence was proclaimed in August 1957 hunger, desertion, wounds, disease, and jungle melancholy had reduced Communist strength to a mere 1,500 men. After independence the Communists no longer had anything to offer. Gradually the Min Yuen was destroyed and they were hunted down. When the Emergency was finally declared over in July 1960 only about 500 remained at large. These fled for the jungles of Thailand. 9,520 had been killed and wounded, 1,287 captured, and 2,702 had surrendered during the course of the struggle. Malayan police casualties were 2,947 and those of the military forces 1,478. Civilian casualties during the Emergency amounted to 4,668. The Communists had been beaten by a combination of aggressive anti-guerrilla tactics, the removal of large sections of the population, the absence of external aid, and the failure to win 'the hearts and minds' of the people. Driven deeper and deeper into the jungle by hunter-killer platoons expertly trained in jungle warfare they became fugitives rather than guerrilla fighters. The Communist uprising, contrary to the teachings of Mao Tse-Tung, ended in dismal failure.

If Mao's tactics failed in Malaya, in Indo-China, however, they resulted in the greatest victory won by a guerrilla army over a colonial power. Here the French, who had attempted to rule through the Emperor Bao Dai, completely failed to understand the meaning of Mao's concept of revolutionary guerrilla war. The French held the big cities of the Red river and Mekong deltas. Beyond these main centres where the Viet Minh ruled they established a string of isolated garrisons. After failing to oust the French, who were superior in numbers and equipment, in 1946 Giap had been driven northward into the hills along the Chinese border where the French then built a line of forts to contain him.

Giap seemed beaten and French attention was then concentrated mainly on the south where Viet Minh terrorists were gaining ground in the villages. In November 1949 the victorious Chinese Communist armies reached the North Vietnamese border and henceforth the Viet Minh were sure of bases, tactical and military aid. A year later they infiltrated the jungle south of the French forts, thus isolating them from the main French army. By 17 October 1950 the forts had surrendered. The French had lost 6,000 men and a large quantity of arms. Encouraged by this success Giap, who now commanded 80 battalions, launched a drive against Hanoi and Haiphong in January 1951. This was blocked by the French commander, General de Lattre de Tassigny, at Vinh Yen, 30 miles north-west of Hanoi. Here napalm and high explosive destroyed Giap's human waves. The French triumphed and the Viet Minh lost 6,500 men. De Tassigny also cut the Viet Minh north–south supply line by the capture of Hoa Binh in November 1951 (see Map 11). The French, although surrounded, held on for four months, inflicting heavy losses upon the Viet Minh. De Tassigny, however, fell ill and Hoa Binh was evacuated a month after his death in January 1952.

A long and frustrating stalemate followed. In the north the guerrillas consistently avoided all French attempts to force a pitched battle. The Vietnamese villager was a peasant by day and a guerrilla by night. General Henri Navarre, who was appointed French commander in Indo-China in May 1953, found to his horror that despite 100,000 French troops in the Red river delta the Viet Minh controlled 5,000 of the area's 7,000 villages. Navarre despaired of complete victory but hoped to fight the enemy to a stand-still and so force an armistice like that in Korea. He was also committed to protect Laos where the Viet Minh had established a kindred Communist organisation, Pathet Lao.

As Giap's forces moved towards an invasion of Laos, Navarre selected the village of Dien Bien Phu, a short distance from the Laotian border, as the place to block the enemy and force him into a decisive battle. On 20 November 1953 an air armada began to parachute 15,000 troops and their equipment including tanks and artillery into Dien Bien Phu to establish a base. It was a strange place to choose since it was 200 miles from Hanoi and could only be supplied and reinforced by air (see Map 11). Bad weather could easily make this more difficult. It was, moreover, a basin completely surrounded by hills and exposed on all sides to artillery fire. While the French prepared their armed camp the Viet Minh divisions were rapidly approaching:

> Covering twenty miles by day or fifty by night. . . . Nothing distinguished the officers from the troops. . . . Each soldier carried his weapon . . . a bag, a 30 lb. bundle of rice . . . his individual shovel, water bottle, and a little salt in a bamboo tube. He marched from dawn to sunset or vice versa with ten minutes rest every hour. . . . On arrival he dug trenches in which to take shelter and sleep after washing his feet in a bowl of hot salt water . . . many . . . had only sandals cut out of tyres. . . .[1]

Navarre, whose resources were limited by the French Treasury, underestimated

[1] Jules Roy, *The Battle of Dien Bien Phu* (Faber), pp. 71-2.

57   Dien Bien Phu. The French start a counter-attack

his enemy from the outset. French Intelligence believed that Giap would be unable to concentrate or feed sufficient troops to capture Dien Bien Phu. Giap, however, kept four Viet Minh divisions supplied by 80,000 coolies who for months wheeled food and munitions through the jungle on bicycles. Suitably reinforced a bicycle could carry a weight of 500 lb. – a greater burden than an elephant could bear. Navarre too believed that Giap lacked heavy guns and the means to transport them to the heights around Dien Bien Phu. Working at night, however, the Viet Minh towed 20 105 mm. guns, 18 75 mm. guns, 80 37 mm. guns, and 100 anti-aircraft guns unobserved through the jungle and onto the heights. Many of these came from the Chinese who had captured them in Korea. The whole population was mobilised to help the Viet Minh. Roads damaged by French bombing were immediately repaired by teams of villagers. Unexploded bombs were detonated by herds of buffalo. Where no roads existed they were built. By January 1954 the French were trapped and surrounded by thousands of guerrillas in palm and bamboo helmets who, cooking in smokeless ovens, were invisible in the jungle.

On 13 March 1954 the guns which the French did not believe existed began their bombardment, pouring 18 shells a minute into Dien Bien Phu while the anti-aircraft guns shot the French transports out of the sky. For the next eight weeks the French defence was ground down. The waves of assault troops were preceded by squads of dynamiters who cleared the barbed wire with bamboo poles stuffed with explosives.

As the world followed the agony of the besieged garrison of Frenchmen, Legionnaires, Vietnamese, and North Africans, John Foster Dulles, American Secretary of State, announced that he was prepared to take the world to 'the brink of war' to stop a Communist victory in Indo-China. Communist success in China and the Korean war had already produced grave American anxiety about Communist expansion in Asia and the safety of the American Pacific defence system. The French appeared to be holding the southern line against Asian communism and by 1954 America was paying 78 per cent of the French cost of the war. On 24 March 1954 Dulles and Admiral Radford, Chairman of the U.S. Joint Chiefs of Staff, proposed to save Dien Bien Phu by an American air strike from the Philippines. 60 B.29 bombers would drop atomic bombs on the hills surrounding the beleaguered base. The idea was stopped by Congress, by British protests, and the difficulties of accurate bombing. Dulles's attempt 'to

call the bluff of Communist China' came to naught. On 7 May the last screaming human wave engulfed the defenders and the survivors of the French garrison surrendered. The fall of Dien Bien Phu, one of the greatest defeats ever suffered by the West, caused utter amazement. With one blow Giap had made French withdrawal from Vietnam inevitable. If the British had won the battle for the minds and bodies of the people of Malaya, the French had lost this battle in Vietnam. Giap's peasant army was determined to conquer and re-possess its own land regardless of sacrifice and cost, a fact which the Americans would have been wise to note.

At a Geneva Peace Conference two months later Vietnam was divided into two parts along the 17th parallel. In the north the Viet Minh was recognised as the legal government. In the south a nationalist régime was established with American backing (see Map 11). Time was allotted for the Vietnamese to travel to their chosen zone. 860,000 refugees crossed from the north to the south. These were mainly Catholics, many of whom had collaborated with the French. At the same time large numbers of Viet Minh guerrillas returned unobtrusively to their southern villages. At Geneva it had been agreed that national elections should be held within two years to reunite Vietnam. This America refused to accept, wishing to keep South Vietnam as a barrier to Communist advance in Asia.

Two months after the Geneva Conference, Dulles in a conference at Manila persuaded Britain, France, Australia, New Zealand, Pakistan, Thailand, the Philippines to join America in a South-East Asia Collective Defence Treaty. The aim of SEATO was to contain communism in the Far East as NATO had done in Europe (see Map 4). India, Burma, and Indonesia, however, refused to join. The Asiatics quickly saw that the most substantial SEATO forces were those of America, who had no territory in Asia. To them it was the Americans, discredited by association with the former colonial powers, who were the intruders and enemies of freedom in Asia and not the Chinese or Russians. Asian suspicions multiplied when America signed a mutual defence treaty with Nationalist China in February 1955. Despite its weaknesses and domination by Western powers SEATO enjoyed some success in that there was no sizeable Communist activity in the treaty area between 1954 and 1961. Neither America nor the world, however, had heard the last of Vietnam.

58   Dien Bien Phu. A helicopter has landed to take off French wounded. A red-cross flag is waved in the hope that the Viet Minh will not fire

59   A French plane has dropped paratroopers inside the fighting perimeter of the Dien Bien Phu fortress

8 The Nuclear Armaments Race

FROM THE BEGINNING of the Cold War the West was haunted by the fear that Russia would one day match America in nuclear armaments. When the American lead in this field ended Russia would be free to take advantage of her great superiority in conventional forces which the West had never attempted to match. America could not be expected to counter a Russian invasion of Western Europe when the American continent was itself open to nuclear attack.

In December 1947 the U.S. Atomic Energy Commission evacuated Eniwetok Atoll in the Marshall Islands to use it as a permanent atomic testing ground. In January 1949 the Americans confidently announced that they possessed bombs of a much greater explosive power than those dropped on Hiroshima and Nagasaki, but in September a detective device in Alaska registered increased radio-activity in the stratosphere. Three years before the West had calculated Russia had exploded an atomic bomb. A deadly race in nuclear armaments had begun.

Russian success was doubtless to some extent due to the work of German atomic scientists who had been captured at the end of the war and to Dr Klaus Fuchs, a leading scientist at the Harwell Atomic Energy Establishment in Britain. Fuchs, a former member of the German Communist Party, who had been given asylum in Britain, was arrested in February 1950 for giving atomic secrets to a Communist 'spy ring' in America which had passed them on to Russia.

Two months later the Americans hinted at progress towards the development of a 'super bomb' one hundred to a thousand times more powerful than the atomic bomb, and in January 1950 President Truman officially sanctioned the manufacture of this hydrogen bomb. By November a plant had been set up in South Carolina to make materials for the H-bomb. Another plant was established in Colorado in March 1951.

Two more Russian bombs were exploded in October 1951, but American progress, hastened by the Korean war, still emphasised her nuclear supremacy. Contracts were placed for the manufacture of the first American atomic submarine in August 1951, and in October Gordon Deane, Chairman of the Atomic Energy Commission, announced after atomic tests in the Nevada Desert that America would soon have as wide a variety of atomic weapons as conventional ones. His statement seemed justified when in May 1952 the prototype was produced of a 75-ton atomic gun capable of hitting a target under any conditions. Six more American bombs were exploded in Nevada tests in the same month when large numbers of American troops were tried in atomic battle conditions. The climax came on 1 November 1952 at Eniwetok Atoll where America exploded her first hydrogen bomb. As the bomb exploded flames 2 miles wide and 5 miles high shot into the air. A pillar of smoke rose for 25 miles and a mushroom cloud formed a hundred miles long. The test island disappeared leaving a hole in the ocean bed 175 feet deep and a mile in diameter. Experts estimated that in a modern city the blast would cover an area of 300 square miles. New York or any of the world's greatest cities could be obliterated by one single bomb. A war with such bombs would destroy civilisation.

60   The hydrogen bomb, November 1952. This photo
was taken at a height of about 12,000 ft and 50 miles
from the detonation site. The mushroom went up to 10
miles and spread for about 100 miles

Once again American nuclear superiority seemed assured for a considerable time.
Not only was Russia open to nuclear attack by long-range B.52 bombers from bases in
America itself but also from medium-range bombers stationed in European NATO
bases and American bases in Iceland, Greenland, Canada, Morocco, the West Indies,
Japan, and the Far East (see Map 8). In 1952 the menacing circle around Russia was
tightened by the admission to NATO of Greece and Turkey. When entry was refused
to Fascist Spain America bought permission to establish bases at Cadiz, Cartagena,
Palma, Seville, and Saragossa in return for several million dollars (see Map 8).

Then the bombshell fell. On 20 August 1953 Russia exploded a hydrogen bomb.
America had been in a state of national emergency since China's entry into the Korean
war. Civil defence for a nuclear war had been organised on a crash basis. In New York
alone 14,000 sky-watchers had been recruited to watch for Russian bombers and a
scheme prepared to evacuate a million women and children to the state of New Jersey.
With Russian possession of the H-bomb the destruction of America by long-range bombing in a war excluding military and naval forces became a very real prospect. Against
such attack there was no defence save counter-attack. The possession of nuclear weapons
thus became a 'deterrent'. American bombers everywhere were placed in a condition of
'high alert' in order that they should not be caught helpless on the ground and should
be ready for 'massive retaliation' in the event of Russian attack. By 1955 Russia possessed
a bomber equivalent to the American B.52 with a range of 6,000 miles. Both sides, too,
had begun to experiment with the production of guided rockets which were less vulner-
able than aircraft and were capable of carrying nuclear warheads across continents.
The Germans had used V2 rockets as a long-distance means of striking at Britain in the

closing stages of World War II. Their V2 rockets now became the basis for further development.

In America Russia's rapid nuclear progress produced a crisis of confidence, which was aggravated by the Communist 'spy rings' uncovered in 1946 and 1947, and the frustrations of the Korean war. Twelve Communist Party leaders were imprisoned in 1951. A 'witch hunt' for Communists followed in the forces, the universities, the civil service, and the schools. This was conducted by Joseph McCarthy, a Republican Senator. By the close of 1953 over 1,450 government employees had been dismissed or had resigned as a result of his denunciations. Books by supposed Communist authors were burned. The Communist Party in America was outlawed in August 1954 but many of McCarthy's victims were liberal-minded Americans who had no Communist sympathies at all. Finally McCarthy went too far and was condemned by the Senate in December 1954 for his activities, but his success was an indication of the panic arising from the fear of the spread of communism in America.

As Russia and America neared nuclear equality it also became obvious that Western Europe could not be defended without rearming western Germany. Not only did the NATO armies require this from a strategic viewpoint but also West German manpower would help offset Russian numerical superiority. West Germany had already been accepted in 1951 as a member of the European Coal and Steel Community which provided a single market in coal and steel for France, Italy, West Germany, and the Benelux countries. Not surprisingly, however, deep hostility to West German rearmament came from France and large sections of British public opinion.

To many Americans, untouched by Hitler's aggression, West Germany was 'America's best friend in Europe'. Western fear of Russia was also greater than that of a revived Germany, and eventually in October 1954 West Germany became the fifteenth member of NATO and a 'free and equal partner of the West'. She was, however, denied the use of nuclear weapons. Her initial contribution to Western defence was 12 army divisions and 12 reserve divisions. Later, ironically, some of her troops were to train in Britain. To Russia and her satellites West German rearmament brought the danger of attempts at German reunification and efforts to regain the lost territories east of the Oder–Neisse Line.

The inevitable and final clash between the two camps which seemed to be so rapidly approaching in the early 1950s did not take place. Instead in the middle fifties there were attempts on both sides to reduce the tension, while the arms race continued accompanied by the daily possibility that a new discovery by either side could completely upset the balance of nuclear power. Both sides were undoubtedly influenced by the crippling costs of nuclear research. To the European members of the Western alliance, likely at any moment to lose American nuclear protection if Russia forged ahead, the need to achieve a Cold War settlement seemed critical to avoid Russian nuclear destruction one by one. Russia, too, had her problems. Despite gloomy predictions in the West she still had insufficient nuclear bombs or bombers by mid-1955 to consider an all-out attack on America. In addition Russia's leaders also had serious problems to solve in both the Soviet Union and her East European empire.

9 The Satellites Revolt

ON 5 MARCH 1953, six months before Russia exploded the H-bomb, Joseph Stalin, Russian dictator since 1929, died of a stroke. As a line of mourners stretched through the Moscow streets for 10 miles waiting to pay homage to their dead leader, the remaining leaders feared internal confusion and Western attack during the power struggle that was to come.

Initially Georgi Malenkov, Secretary of the Russian Communist Party, became Prime Minister. Within a fortnight, however, he was obliged to give up the Party Secretariat to Nikita Khrushchev, a clear sign that he was not unanimously accepted as Stalin's successor. Stalin had ruled Russia with an iron hand. Even his closest associates had not been safe from the danger of his party purges and executions. The Russian leaders were not only jealous of each other but determined that there should be no repetition of Stalin's brutal tyranny. The man they most feared was Beria, Stalin's principal lieutenant and head of Russia's $1\frac{1}{2}$ million secret police. When Beria, a Georgian like Stalin, was suspected of preparing a *coup* he was arrested and shot by his colleagues in June 1953. The secret police then passed under the control of a Party Committee to make it more difficult for them to become the instrument of any one man. Large numbers of prisoners were released from labour camps and there was a general softening of Russian life. Against this background the power struggle between Malenkov and Khrushchev continued.

In February 1955 Malenkov 'resigned' the premiership and was replaced by Bulganin. He was not, however, liquidated as unsuccessful competitors for power had been in the past. After this triumph Khrushchev's fortunes flourished until at the Party Congress in February 1956 he dumbfounded both the Communist and non-Communist worlds with a dramatic denunciation of Stalin. Among other things Stalin was condemned for replacing collective leadership by dictatorship; for his fostering of a 'personality

61   March 1953. Soviet leaders and foreign Communist guests follow Stalin's coffin. *Right to left*: Khrushchev, Chou En-Lai (*third from right*), Malenkov, Voroshilov, Kaganovitch, Bulganin, Molotov

cult'; and his brutal and unjust repression of opposition. He was charged also with failure to prepare for the German invasion in 1941 and for the breach with Yugoslavia in 1948. Stalin's corpse was removed from the Mausoleum in Red Square where it had been placed with such ceremony beside that of Lenin, and reburied in obscurity. The surviving victims of his purges in the thirties were released. Those who had been executed were posthumously rehabilitated.

Khrushchev's stock rose with 'de-Stalinisation'. In June 1957 Malenkov, Molotov, and Kaganovitch, his principal rivals, were dismissed as deputy premiers and removed from the Party Central Committee. His supremacy was formally recognised in March 1958 when he replaced Bulganin as Prime Minister and became leader of both the government and the Party. He never, however, became an absolute dictator as Stalin had been. The deliberate destruction of the cult of Stalin made it impossible for his tyranny to be copied.

In these circumstances Russia could not afford to risk any major international crisis between 1953 and 1958. She therefore hastened to secure a *détente* or lowering of international tension. Western powers, especially Britain, in the light of Russia's rapid nuclear advance were prepared to comply. The signing of the Korean armistice in July 1953 was the first indication of a changing attitude. In January 1954 the Council of Foreign Ministers met for the first time in five years to discuss the problem of Germany. The West wanted free elections and the right of an independent Germany to follow its own foreign policy and join NATO if it wished. The Russians on the other hand wanted to neutralise Germany and provide an area of disengagement in Central Europe. They obviously could not accept a NATO power on the Polish border. No agreement was reached but the rival governments were at least again on speaking terms. At the Geneva Conference in April 1954 a settlement was achieved for the time being in Indo-China. In May 1955 Russia signed an Austrian peace treaty and withdrew her troops from Austria. Bulganin and Khrushchev also recognised the Federal German Republic, although now a NATO member. The West, perhaps unwisely, clung to the idea of a united Germany and refused recognition to Herr Ulbricht's East German régime. Khrushchev's attempts to achieve 'peaceful co-existence' of the rival blocs culminated in the Geneva Summit Conference of July 1955 when the American, British, French, and Russian leaders met for four days to prepare an

62 The Soviet Communist Party 20th Congress, 1956. Delegates listen to Khrushchev's speech denouncing Stalin

63 The Big Four Summit, 1955: Bulganin, Eisenhower, Faure, Eden

agenda for more detailed negotiations by the four Foreign Ministers. The Summit aroused high hopes in Western Europe. Left to themselves President Eisenhower and Khrushchev, who both tended towards conciliation, may have enjoyed some success. When the Foreign Ministers' Conference met in October John Foster Dulles and Molotov ensured that it failed. Dulles stood for the liberation of China and Eastern Europe. Molotov, formerly Stalin's chief negotiator, who remained Foreign Minister until the summer of 1956, was equally tough and uncompromising.

In addition to Russia's complex internal political situation there was another good reason for the Russians to reduce international tension in the middle-fifties. The Russian empire that Stalin had so painstakingly built in Eastern Europe had become dangerously over-extended. It was seething with economic discontent and frustrated national feeling, and appeared likely at any moment to break away. After 1949, when all political independence was lost, Russia had exploited her satellite states like colonies. The expectations of socialist development had not materialised. Large amounts of food and goods went to Russia as reparations. Socialism had brought instead forced labour, purges, and deportation. Peasants were forced to amalgamate the land they had so recently received into big and often unsuccessful collective farms. After the outbreak of the Korean war matters worsened. Countries which had been shattered by World War II were expected to increase industrial and agricultural production for another war. Living standards fell instead of rising, because of the shortage of food and consumer goods. Increased demands from peasants and industrial workers produced apathy and sometimes resistance. This in turn led to greater secret police activity, arrests, and deportation to labour camps. The Russian occupation forces became increasingly hated by workers, students, and intellectuals alike. Russia's difficulties with national communism had begun as early as 1948 when Tito and Yugoslavia had broken from the Cominform. Everything Yugoslavia had said about Stalin's intentions and their consequences now seemed correct.

Signs of trouble first appeared with strikes and riots at Pilsen in Czechoslovakia in 1953, which were suppressed by local police. A more critical situation, however, developed in East Germany where on 1 May 1953 ration cards were withdrawn from large sections of the middle class. On 16 June 3,000 East Berlin building-workers downed tools in protest against new working 'norms' which required them to do 10 per cent more

64 John Foster Dulles, the uncompromising U.S. Secretary of State, famous for his brinkmanship

65 June 1953. Russian tanks patrol East Berlin streets watched by hostile crowds

work without any wage increase. Joined by large crowds they demonstrated outside the East German government headquarters for the abolition of the 'norms' and the People's Police, free elections, and increased rations. Next day further demonstrations occurred. Thousands of railway- and factory-workers and employees in the public services marched again with large sections of the population to the government offices. Their cries now included greater political and economic freedom, union with West Germany, the end of communism, and the withdrawal of Russian forces. As the People's Police lost control of the situation Russian tanks, armoured cars, and infantry were called out to restore order. The Eastern zone was sealed off from the rest of Berlin and when tanks were stoned police and Russian troops fired on the crowds. A curfew and martial law were declared, to last for nearly a month.

Similar strikes and riots occurred in a number of other East German cities. At Magdeburg a factory was burned down and pitched battles fought between demonstrators and People's Police. 25 people were killed and 378 injured. Reports of arrests and executions by the Russian authorities followed. 300,000 refugees fled during 1953 from the Eastern zone to the West including many People's Police, disgusted at the repression of the rising. The 'norms', however, were withdrawn, ration cards were returned, and a considerable number of economic concessions granted to the East Germans by a frightened government. In August 1953 the Russians in turn announced sizeable economic concessions to East Germany. Reparations which had proved such a drain on the East German economy were cancelled; industries confiscated by Russia after the war were returned to the East German government. Soviet occupation costs were drastically reduced. On 25 March 1954 Russia recognised East Germany as an 'independent state conducting its own internal and external affairs'. The Soviet Union had received a sharp lesson.

From the summer of 1953 to the close of 1955 Russia's economic exactions from the other satellite nations were also reduced. Since the Soviet empire was too large to control by force there was a conscious bid to win over the subject peoples. In May 1955 after seven years of conflict with Yugoslavia Khrushchev himself visited Tito in an attempt to heal the breach. In the same month Russia concluded the Warsaw Pact, a 20-year treaty of 'friendship, co-operation and mutual assistance' with Poland, Czechoslovakia, East Germany, Hungary, Romania, Bulgaria, and Albania. China signed as an associate. The pact, made as a result of West German rearmament, established a unified military command for the forces of the countries concerned under Marshal Koniev, one of Russia's leading soldiers in World War II (see Map 4). Having bound her satellites to her by treaty on 17 April 1956 Russia dissolved the Cominform. She could no longer hope to dictate to the other Communist parties in the way that Stalin had done and was prepared to accept their nominal independence and equality while they remained loyal to the Warsaw Pact and to Russia. The West no longer faced one giant empire rigidly controlled from Moscow but it was extremely slow to realise this. This relaxation of control combined with the impact of de-Stalinisation upon the Communist bloc had the completely opposite effect to that which was intended. With greater freedom, anti-Soviet national ferment only increased. In his attempts at reform Khrushchev had released forces beyond his control and two of his satellites almost broke away.

Khrushchev's denunciation of Stalin had immediate repercussions in the satellite states. The Stalinist Bulgarian Prime Minister, Chervenkov, resigned and Kostov, a Bulgarian Communist Party Secretary executed for treason in 1949, was posthumously rehabilitated. While the East German premier Herr Grotewohl criticised justice in East Germany during the Stalinist régime, vice-premier Walter Ulbricht attacked Stalin himself. Elsewhere criticism of Communist Party abuses, policies, and officials in Eastern Europe during Stalin's lifetime was equally strong. Large numbers of political prisoners were released in Bulgaria, Hungary, Poland, and Czechoslovakia.

In Poland Wladyslaw Gomulka, a wartime Communist resistance leader and former vice-premier, was released from prison and reinstated on 6 April 1956. Gomulka had been expelled from the Polish Communist Party in 1949 and imprisoned in 1951 on charges of 'Titoism'. He had in other words objected to the direction of the Polish Communist state by Stalin, and the subordination of its interests to Russia. 30,000 other Polish political prisoners were released in the amnesty. As the Stalinists were dismissed from the Polish Cabinet restrictions were placed upon the hated security police and

66   The signing of the Warsaw Pact. *Seated,* Molotov, Marshal Zhukov. *Standing at the back*: Rokossovsky, Cyrankiewicz (Poland); Ulbricht, Stoph (E. Germany); Hegedus, Bata (Hungary)

67   November 1956. Gomulka (*centre*) and Prime Minister Cyrankiewicz (*left*) return from Moscow where they have confirmed Poland's new policies

proposals were made for greater democracy in economic and political life with increased parliamentary control over the government. Nationalism, however, had always been strong in Poland. There was, moreover, widespread dissatisfaction with low wages, poor living conditions, and high prices. On 28 June the return of a workers' delegation from the Zispo engineering works, which had unsuccessfully travelled to Warsaw to put its case to the government, was the signal for serious rioting in Poznan. Thousands of factory-workers carrying Polish flags left their factories and converged on the main square. They attacked the Communist Party headquarters and a radio station, set fire to the prison, and released a number of prisoners. Many were armed with rifles

68   The popular Imre Nagy with admirers during the Hungarian revolution

69   Hungarians burn Russian literature and propaganda

made at the Zispo works or given them by sympathetic soldiers. The first troops to appear fraternised with the strikers and ominously joined in the battle against the security police. Polish army tanks and infantry reinforcements were rushed to Poznan where all communications with the outside world had ceased. By evening order was restored. 53 people including nine soldiers and security police were dead and 300 were wounded. The Ministers of the Motor and Engineering Industries were relieved of their posts together with the head of the Economic Planning Commission. £500,000 in taxes which had been 'unjustly collected' from the Zispo workers were refunded. Many of those arrested were later released.

Polish unrest, however, was far from over. At a three-day Central Committee meeting of the Polish Communist Party on 19–21 October the remaining Stalinists were dismissed. These included Marshal Rokossovsky, the Minister of Defence, who had spent most of his life in Russia, distinguished himself in World War II, and afterwards re-adopted Polish nationality. Gomulka, only recently re-admitted to party membership after five years in jail, was unanimously elected First Secretary of the Party. From the speeches made it was clear that he and his colleagues were determined to continue the advance towards democracy in Polish economic and political life. They were also determined that Poland, while continuing a policy of alliance with Russia, should follow her own road to socialism and resist any Soviet attempt to dominate her internal affairs. In emphasising the many different roads to socialism they constantly pointed to the example of Yugoslavia.

During the first day of the session the proceedings were dramatically interrupted by the arrival of the Russian leaders Khrushchev, Molotov, Mikoyan, and Kaganovitch who had flown unannounced from Moscow. They feared that Gomulka, the 'Polish Tito', intended to break away from Russia altogether. If this happened Russia's link with East Germany would be cut. East Germany would rejoin the Federal German Republic and Russia would again face a united Germany. This it could not allow. The Central Committee meeting was suspended as the Russian and Polish leaders conferred for many hours. As they talked Russian tanks from Silesia began to move on Warsaw, and Polish army units positioned themselves to defend the city. There were, however, no clashes. Gomulka satisfied the Russians that he would not break away. They and the

70   25 October. Russian tanks move
into Budapest to quell the Hungarian
rising

71   30 October. A silent crowd watch the
body of an AVH man, lynched and
burnt outside Party HQ

tanks withdrew, and in return for a guarantee of loyalty Poland secured a limited independence and liberty of action.

In Hungary a similar crisis took place but Imre Nagy, the 'Hungarian Tito', was not able to control the nation as Gomulka had done. In consequence a nationalist revolution broke out which ended in a bloodbath. Until 1949 Hungary had prospered under communism. Living standards rose above the pre-war level; working conditions improved, unemployment vanished, and the land was shared among the peasantry. After 1949 with the Stalinists under Matyas Rakosi in complete control Hungary was treated as a Russian colony. A Russian-type Five Year Plan began to develop heavy industry at the expense of consumer goods and the peasants were forced to join collective farms. Exports of food to East Germany ordered by the Russians brought severe food shortages. Production norms were increased in industry and 'peace loans' levied on the workers. Opposition brought a Stalinist reign of terror by Rakosi's secret police (AVH) and mass deportations to mines and labour camps.

With Stalin's death Malenkov replaced Rakosi as premier by the more moderate Imre Nagy. Nagy had joined the Russian Red Army when a prisoner in 1917. After a brief part in the Hungarian Communist government of 1919 he had spent most of his life in Russia, returning with the Soviet army to become Minister of Agriculture in the post-war Communist government. He condemned the 'mistakes of the past' and between 1953 and 1955 allowed peasants to leave the collective farms and return to private farming. When Malenkov fell in 1955 Khrushchev, fearing trouble in Hungary, brought back the tougher Rakosi to power. Nagy was expelled from the Party as a 'Titoist'. After his more lenient régime Rakosi's ruthless methods soon aroused bitter opposition, especially when he began to force the peasants back to collective farms. In July 1956 he resigned but was replaced by his lieutenant, Erno Gero. Nagy, however, was rehabilitated and returned to political life. A number of other rehabilitated Hungarian Communists executed for 'Titoism' in 1949 were given a state reburial. The news of Gomulka's reinstatement and success in Poland immediately caused Hungarians to expect the right to run their own affairs. On 22–23 October hundreds of thousands of workers, students, and soldiers demonstrated in Budapest and other Hungarian cities, calling for more democracy, the withdrawal of Russian forces, the removal of Stalinists, and the return of Nagy to power. Heavy fighting broke out in Budapest on the night of 23–24 October. Hungarian soldiers tore the Soviet stars from their caps and joined the demonstrators in an attack on Budapest radio station which was defended by the AVH. The rebels established themselves on Csepel Island, an industrial area south of Budapest, and attacked Communist and government buildings and the military barracks. A state of emergency was declared throughout Hungary; all rail and air communications were cut with the outside world. At 7 a.m. on 24 October Nagy was appointed Prime Minister but eight hours later Gero, invoking the Warsaw Pact, called in Russian troops to restore order.

By 25 October large portions of western Hungary were in rebel hands and two insurgent radio stations were on the air. It was evident that many soldiers of the Hungarian regular army had joined the industrial workers and even supplied them with arms. Nagy admitted the grievances of the rebels and promised to form a new government to rectify them. Gero was replaced as Party Secretary by Janos Kadar who had been imprisoned for 'Titoism' in 1950. By this time, as fighting continued, over 150 Russian tanks had arrived in Budapest:

> Tanks blocked the main Danube bridges and covered all principal cross-roads. Burnt-out lorries and cars lay on their sides in the street. Broken glass glistened on the pavements and the smashed cable wires of the tram system trailed on the ground. From blackened doors came that acrid war-time smell of debris mingled with spent gun fire and corpses.[1]

When tanks opened fire on a crowd in Parliament Square women and children were mown down and over a hundred people killed. Elsewhere the tanks were used as 'extermination squads', rumbling from one district to another and flattening every house suspected of concealing snipers. In response to workers' demands for the withdrawal of Russian troops Nagy secured a promise to this effect from the Soviet commander on 28 October. He also promised to disband the AVH, who in many places had been lynched when captured. On 30 October the Russians began to leave Budapest but as they did so Nagy declared the end of the one-party system and the formation of a national government based on the Communist Party, the Social Democrats, the Smallholders, and the National Peasant Party. The whole character of the revolution had changed. Nagy could no longer restrain Hungarian nationalism and its bitter hatred of communism and the Russians. Red, white, and green flags fluttered in the streets and on 1 November he announced Hungary's withdrawal from the Warsaw Pact and appealed to the U.N. and the Great Powers to guarantee her permanent neutrality.

While the Russians were prepared to accept nominal Hungarian independence provided that she stayed loyal to Moscow, they could allow neither free elections, which would mean an end to communism, nor a total withdrawal from the Communist bloc. If Hungary went, the other East European states, where the situation was already delicate, would follow. Russia's protective empire would collapse and Germany would be reunited with the NATO nations. The Russian withdrawal halted. Reinforcements poured across the Russian and Romanian frontiers and encircled Budapest. Other Russian tanks pressed into western Hungary. The Hungarian appeal to the West fell on deaf ears. Britain and France were already embroiled in the Suez affair and in any

[1] Quoted from the *Daily Telegraph* in Keesing's Contemporary Archives, p. 15190.

case were powerless to intervene. Hungarian government troops took up defensive positions around their capital. On the night of 3–4 November Nagy's Defence Minister and Chief of Staff were seized by the Russians while attempting to negotiate, and at dawn on 4 November a massive attack was launched by Russian tanks and infantry. Budapest Radio for two hours made desperate appeals for U.N. assistance in five languages before it finally went off the air with the words 'Help Hungary . . . help us. . . .'

The Hungarian army, workers, and students fiercely resisted from street barricades the Russian infantry attacking the Parliament building, Danube bridges, railway stations, and factories. Russian tanks were met with improvised petrol bombs flung by men, women, and even children. By 10 November the revolt in the provinces was crushed but in Budapest resistance continued, the rebels preferring to die rather than surrender.

> The repression of Budapest [wrote the *Times* correspondent] was carried out by . . . tanks supported by infantry . . . and self-propelling guns. Their tactics were to neutralise resistance strongpoints with heavy concentrations of fire leaving the rest of the city, apart from tank patrols . . . much to itself.[1]

Food supplies were prevented from reaching the city by the Russians, and as ammunition failed famine threatened. Large numbers of civilians were slaughtered by tank and artillery fire. Tanks fired upon bread queues while some Hungarian soldiers who surrendered were taken to Rakoczi Square and shot. Russian brutality only served,

[1] Keesing's Contemporary Archives, p. 15193.

72 Hungarian revolutionaries remove Lenin's portrait from the Law Courts in Budapest

however, to prolong the fighting. The Hungarians retreated into the narrow alleys where tanks could not penetrate and only with great difficulty did Russian infantry drive them out. By 11 November, however, resistance was over. Only ruin and desolation remained. 25,000 Hungarians were killed and 50,000 wounded in Budapest alone. 3,500 Russians also died in the fighting. A new Communist government was formed under Janos Kadar who had defected to the Russians when they arrived. Nagy took shelter in the Yugoslav embassy but was tricked into leaving his refuge by a promise of safe-conduct from Kadar. He was later taken to Romania and shot. 140,000 refugees streamed out of Hungary, passing mostly into Austria before spreading throughout the world. These were the fortunate ones who escaped before the People's Tribunals established to deal with 'counter-revolutionaries' could begin their work. 200,000 Russian troops, 4,600 tanks, and 2,000 aircraft had kept Hungary in the Soviet bloc and Russia's protective barrier intact.

Before the Hungarian revolution many Eastern Europeans, particularly the older generation who could not easily adapt themselves to communism, had still cherished the hope of liberation by the West. After 1956 this hope was ended and they realised that the West would not risk a nuclear war to aid them. They therefore reluctantly came to terms with communism, which grew gradually stronger. In Hungary, as elsewhere, once proceedings against the counter-revolutionaries had been completed a new calm appeared and living standards slowly improved although still lagging behind the West. The communism which thrived, however, was the more moderate variety of Khrushchev. There was, wisely, no return to the repression of Stalinism. By this time, however, the Cold War had entered two new spheres.

73 Budapest, 19 November, a shattered
city back in the Russian grip

74 Hungarian refugees arrive at the
reception centre at Traiskirchen Castle,
25 miles from Vienna

10 The Cold War Enters the Middle East and Africa

THE MIDDLE EAST at the close of World War II was still an area of Anglo-French influence. Arab nationalism, born in World War I, emerged in 1945 greatly strengthened and determined to free the Arab states from British and French control. To this end a League of Arab states was formed in March 1945 consisting of Egypt, Iraq, Syria, Lebanon, Jordan, Saudi Arabia, and Yemen. Both powers were partially prepared to release countries which were becoming an economic and military burden but were not prepared to leave completely because of their vital oil interests. France gave up her mandates in Syria and the Lebanon in 1944. Britain released Transjordan in 1946 and on 14 May 1948 surrendered her mandate in Palestine before any effective solution had been found to the strife between Jews and Arabs. Since World War I, encouraged by conflicting British war-time promises, both Arabs and Jews had tried to establish a national state in Palestine. By 1936 the situation had deteriorated into civil war which the British could not stop. Originally the Arabs had been in the majority but Nazi persecution in the thirties and the displacement of Jews in World War II had brought large numbers of Jewish immigrants to the 'national home' backed financially from America. Immediately the British left the Jews proclaimed the independent state of Israel. The following day forces of the Arab League invaded Israel. The Israelis seemed doomed but not only were the Arab armies grossly inefficient, the Arab states and their rulers were deeply divided amongst themselves. As a result, when an armistice was concluded in January 1949, apart from a Jordanian sector in the east and the Egyptian-held Gaza strip, the Jews possessed the rest of Palestine (see Map 7).

The Arab humiliation and defeat produced bitter hostility towards Britain for not handing Palestine to the Arabs; and created also a widespread demand for Arab unity and regeneration, and in some cases for political and social revolution. After 1945 Russian prestige in the area was high. The Russian government was not involved in the political issues and appeared to be no threat save perhaps to Iran and Turkey (see Map 7). To many young intellectuals emerging with the slow spread of education, Russian-type planning and industrialisation seemed the answer to the grinding poverty and backwardness of the Arab states.

In April 1951 British prestige suffered a severe blow when the Iranian government led by Dr Mossadeq withdrew the concession it had made to the Anglo-Iranian Oil Company in 1933 by nationalising the industry and seizing the Abadan refinery. A settlement was eventually reached in 1953 after Mossadeq's fall from power but a move in 1951 by Britain, Turkey, and France to set up a Middle East Defence Organisation in co-operation with the Arab states met with no success.

In Egypt, too, anti-British feeling grew more violent. In October 1951 the Egyptian government not only denounced the proposed Middle East Defence Organisation but called for a British evacuation of the Canal zone and the Sudan. These demands strengthened after July 1952 when the corrupt government of King Farouk was overthrown by a group of young army officers. The new régime, led initially by General Neguib and later by Colonel Abdel Nasser, cleaned up government administration and introduced some land reform. By combining nationalism and state socialism, a formula

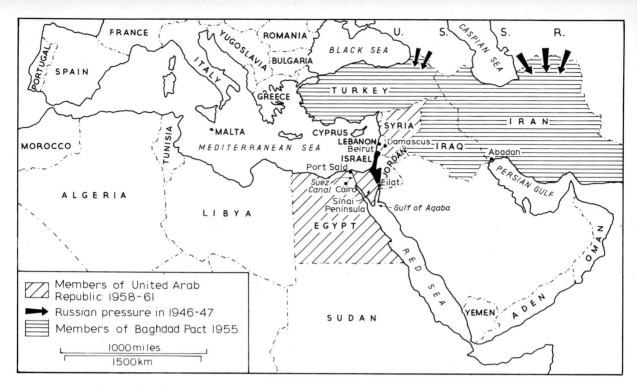

to be copied in other Arab states, Nasser soon won the support of the discontented masses. In February 1953 Britain agreed upon self-government for the Sudan and in October 1954, despite bitter opposition from some of its own members, Churchill's Conservative government agreed to withdraw British troops from the Suez base, believing it unnecessary in a nuclear age.

To seal the gap, however, between NATO and SEATO, protect her interests in the Middle East, and contain Russia, Britain joined with Iraq, Turkey, Pakistan, and Iran in the Baghdad Pact, later called the Central Treaty Organisation (CENTO) (see Map 4). America, although not joining, kept in close contact with the alliance which was formed between January and October 1955. The pact was received with little enthusiasm. Iraq's Prime Minister, Nuri es-Said, had to crush a popular protest, and throughout the Arab world it was condemned as an instrument of 'Western imperialism' and an obstacle to Arab unity. In Egypt, Nasser, as the most powerful leader in the Arab world, was particularly critical. He was committed not only to anti-imperialism but also to Arab unity. But the only cause upon which the Arabs would unite was the destruction of Israel and to this end he now turned. America had caused Britain to yield over the Suez base to win Egyptian support in the Cold War. She would not, however, supply arms to Nasser because of the strong Jewish support for Israel in America. Nasser therefore turned for his arms to the Communist camp.

It is surprising that Russia had not interfered more actively in the Middle East in the post-war years. After her pressure upon Iran and Turkey in 1946–7 she had withdrawn almost completely to consolidate her gains in Eastern Europe. In the Stalinist era, too, the middle-class Arab nationalist leaders had been regarded with suspicion by the Russians who thought it essential to form Arab Communist parties to carry through successful revolution. After Stalin's death, however, the new Russian leaders were more prepared to aid any common enemies of the West, and by 1955 the Cold War had entered the Middle East.

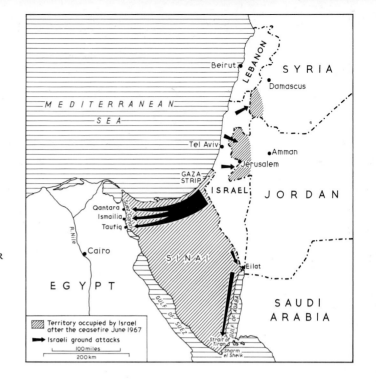

THE ARAB-ISRAELI FIVE-DAY WAR
Over a decade of uneasy peace
followed Suez but the Middle East
again erupted into war in June
1967 (*see pages* 112–14).

In April the Russians condemned the Baghdad Pact; in July the Russian Foreign Minister, Dimitri Shepilov, visited Cairo. By September Nasser was able to announce a £150 million arms purchase from Russia while Syria and the Lebanon also announced a desire for closer co-operation with the Soviet Union. Faced with the danger of Communist penetration into the Middle East, and Egypt becoming a Russian puppet, Britain and America on 17 December 1955 offered financial assistance to Egypt in building the Aswan Dam as part of a large-scale economic development project. Egypt accepted the offer on 17 July 1956 but three days later it was suddenly withdrawn. Nasser presumably had failed to accept the Western terms, while his Russian arms purchase was too much for powerful Jewish sentiment in America. His response was to nationalise the internationally owned Suez Canal Company to obtain money for the dam. The West was caught by surprise. The Canal not only linked Britain with her remaining Far Eastern empire but carried all the petroleum from the Persian Gulf to Western Europe.

The British Labour government had been accused of weakness over Abadan in 1951. The Conservative government of 1956, despite the absence of support from America, where a Presidential election was in progress, decided upon strong action. It found willing allies in France and Israel. France, too, was concerned for its oil and angered by Nasser's encouragement of Algerian rebellion. Israel was threatened with extermination by Egypt, Syria, and Jordan. Not only had Nasser closed the Canal to Israel but he had also closed the Straits of Tiran to all shipping bound for Eilat, Israel's only port on the Gulf of Aqaba. For years Egyptian commandos had been launching raids into Israeli territory. On 29 October the Israeli army invaded Egypt. Despite its recently acquired Russian equipment the Egyptian army was resoundingly beaten. One section of the Israeli army advanced westward across the Sinai Desert towards the Suez Canal while another advancing northwards cut off the Gaza Strip from the Sinai Peninsula. By 2 November the latter had been completely captured. Two days later the Gulf of Aqaba was reopened. Great quantities of Russian weapons were captured by the Israelis. Meanwhile on 30 October Britain and France demanded that both Egypt and Israel should withdraw their forces 10 miles from the Canal and cease hostilities. They also demanded that Egypt should permit the Anglo-French occupation of key points along the Canal to separate the belligerents and ensure the safety of shipping. The scheme was an obvious conspiracy to re-establish international control of the waterway. The Israelis, who were nowhere near the Canal, immediately accepted the ultimatum. The Egyptians, who had the only forces near to it, refused.

75 October 1948. Israeli infantry attack during the Battle of Gaza

76 Jerusalem, 1949. Lt.-Col. Moshe Dayan (*second from right*) arranging the release of Arab prisoners-of-war with the Arab Legion Commander of Jerusalem

An intensive bombardment of Egyptian airfields by British and French planes from Cyprus and Malta then followed from 31 October to 4 November. Egypt's Russian planes were destroyed on the ground. British and French paratroop and commando landings followed in the Port Said area on 5 November, and after heavy fighting Port Said and Port Fuad were taken the following day. The war in the Middle East immediately caused a world crisis, which in the circumstances of the Cold War brought an instant threat to world peace. The British and French action was greeted with worldwide protest. In Britain the nation was clearly divided. Two Conservative Ministers resigned and the 'Suez Affair' was condemned by Conservatives as well as the Labour Party and large sections of the country. African and Asian members of the Commonwealth protested violently about what appeared to be an old-style imperialist war. No support was forthcoming from America, which in the United Nations sponsored a resolution passed by a large majority calling for a cease-fire. In Syria and Saudi Arabia, Western oil pipelines were blown up. Russia, busily engaged in crushing the Hungarian revolution, was at first slow to react but on 5 November protest letters to Britain and France threatened the use of rockets in support of the Egyptians. This was followed by the threat of Soviet and Chinese 'volunteers'. In the face of such widespread opposition the Anglo-French force had no alternative but to comply with the U.N.

cease-fire resolution. Fighting stopped on 6 November and a U.N. force entered Egypt to take over as Israeli, British, and French forces withdrew.

The whole affair was a colossal Western blunder. Nasser, despite the humiliation of his armies by Israel, became the hero of the Arab world who had bravely resisted the Western 'colonialists'. Russia gained tremendous prestige not only in the Middle East but among Asians and Africans as the nation that had saved Egypt from the 'imperialists' with her rocket threat. The ruthless suppression of the Hungarian revolt was forgotten. Anglo-American relations were severely strained. America had helped to cause the crisis

77   Tehran, 1951. Mossadeq (*right*) in discussions with Seyyed Kashani, religious leader of the extreme Iranian nationalists

78   Dimitri Shepilov (*left*) Russian Foreign Minister, and President Nasser (*right*)

by withdrawing aid for the Aswan Dam and then had deserted her ally. As a result Communist influence was firmly entrenched in the Middle East, bringing with it a series of recurrent crises.

In an attempt to repair the damage, America in November 1956 announced that it would support the independence of the Baghdad Pact states, and on 5 March 1957 promised military and economic aid to those states who needed it in defence against communism. This 'Eisenhower Doctrine', which was condemned by Syria and Egypt, was, however, much less effective than the Truman Doctrine a decade earlier. Already Russia was offering financial and military aid to the Arab states and buying their goods at higher prices than those in world markets. Early in 1957 the Lebanon accepted Eisenhower's offer but Arabs noted that this coincided with a display of air power from the American aircraft-carrier *Forrestal* at Beirut. Jordan, too, accepted but not until King Hussein had dismissed his Prime Minister and cabinet. Only the swift arrival of the American 6th Fleet in the eastern Mediterranean in April 1957 prevented a rising against him in Amman inspired by Egypt and Syria.

Another crisis seemed imminent in August 1957 when President Eisenhower announced that Syria had fallen under Communist influence and it was reported that great numbers of Russian volunteers were arriving there. The American envoy to

79   Sinai, November 1956. Israeli trucks
advance towards Suez

80   November 1956. British troops
march through Port Said

Turkey was refused admission to Syria, who proclaimed that Turkish troops were gathering along her frontiers ready to invade. On 10 September this statement was supported by Russia, who issued an official warning to the Turkish government. Turkey was a member of NATO and the Baghdad Pact, and a world crisis again appeared likely. Neither side, however, was prepared to precipitate the crisis and tension eased.

The respite was temporary. In July 1958 another crisis arose with a Syrian-inspired revolution in the Lebanon against President Chamoun, who had accepted the Eisenhower Doctrine. The U.S. Fleet again hastened to the eastern Mediterranean and British troops were hurriedly flown to Cyprus. While the West claimed that Russian-inspired aggression was being planned against the Lebanon and Jordan from Syria, Russia claimed that the West was preparing to aid the Lebanon, Jordan, and Iraq to invade Syria and then turn south upon Egypt. The latter was rendered impossible on the night of 14 July when a revolution led by General Kassim took place in Iraq. The pro-Western King Feisal and his pro-British Prime Minister, Nuri es-Said, were murdered. To America this was a case of indirect aggression by Russia and on 15 July American marines from the 6th Fleet landed at Beirut to defend the Lebanon. Two days later British troops arrived in Jordan from Cyprus to prevent a similar rebellion there. The situation was stabilised and as it became obvious that the crisis was partly the result of the Arabs' own chronic internal rivalries the British and American troops left. Iraq, however, withdrew from the Baghdad Pact in 1959 and in consequence the alliance was rechristened CENTO.

Neither Russia nor the West had made much headway in their competition for Arab support in face of the Arabs' own rivalries. Between 1959 and 1963 comparative peace reigned in the Middle East as Egypt, Syria, and Iraq struggled for leadership of the Arab world. In September 1961 Syria withdrew from the United Arab Republic which she had formed with Egypt in 1958. Kassim in Iraq began to rival Nasser as supreme Arab leader. Then in February 1963 a group of army officers who shared Nasser's beliefs in 'Arab unity' and 'Arab socialism' murdered Kassim and established a new Iraqi government which expressed a desire to co-operate with Egypt. A month later a military plot in Damascus produced a new Syrian government with the same purpose. Trouble was again brewing which would bring fresh opportunities in the Cold War. Before this happened, however, the power conflict with its attendant dangers had switched to another new sphere – this time that of Africa.

81 November 1956. A column of smoke
rises from Port Said oil-storage depots
fired by Anglo-French forces during
their assault on Suez

82 July 1958. American marines land
on the beach at Beirut, Lebanon

In the French-held provinces of North Africa the same spirit of anti-colonialism
and desire for independence that had appeared in the Middle and Far East had spread
rapidly after World War II. Morocco and Tunisia had been released after some bloodshed in 1956. Algeria had a large, long-established French population, besides rich oil
and mineral deposits, and the French were reluctant to leave it. Encouraged by Egypt
the Algerian nationalists formed the *Front de la Libération Nationale* (FLN) which from
1954 fought a savage guerrilla war against the French for the next eight years. 500,000
French soldiers failed to crush the FLN. When the French government proposed to
negotiate, the French army and the colonists in Algeria rebelled and brought about
the collapse of the Fourth Republic and the return of General de Gaulle. De Gaulle,
despite further rebellions by the French colonists, finally negotiated a settlement which
gave Algeria its independence in March 1962. The Cold War had little direct influence
upon the Algerian revolt, although the FLN received Russian arms from Nasser and a
number of the FLN were Algerians captured in Indo-China and trained by the Viet
Minh. Algeria's first Prime Minister, the left-wing anti-colonialist Ben Bella, however,
was pledged to create an Arab socialist state in Algeria, and although he banned the
Communist Party he had soon established a close relationship with Russia. His successor,
Colonel Boumedienne, who overthrew him in June 1965, pursued similar ends.

The struggles of Arab nationalism had a vital influence upon the region south of
the Sahara. In 1945 only Liberia and Ethiopia were independent in this vast area and
the European imperial powers considered that it would be a long time before 'Black
Africa', with its small educated class, was ready for self-government. The Africans,
however, with the examples of India, Burma, Tunisia, Morocco, and the Suez affair
before them, considered imperialism was collapsing and de-colonisation swept like a
whirlwind across Africa. In 1957 Britain withdrew from the Gold Coast which was
renamed Ghana; France left Guinea the following year, and in 1960 16 African colonial
territories containing 85 million people were released. Within the next three years the
rest of Negro Africa had followed, save for the Union of South Africa, Southern Rhodesia,
and the Spanish and Portuguese colonies. Only Great Britain had planned for the
time when these lands should be granted independence. Some of the other territories
managed to establish orderly governments but this was not the case with the Belgian
Congo which on 30 June 1960 was suddenly released by the Belgian government without
any preparation for self-government.

95

The Congo was three times the size of Western Europe. A land of jungle and savannah, its inhabitants consisted of warring primitive peoples, including pygmies. All its economic resources, including copper and uranium, were concentrated in the southern province of Katanga. The Congolese had suffered badly under the Belgians and there was bitter anti-European hostility. When the Belgians left an explosive situation developed which brought the Cold War for the first time into Black Africa. On 1 July tribal war broke out in the capital of Leopoldville. Four days later the Congolese army mutinied and as anarchy spread European families fled to escape the atrocities of the uncontrolled soldiers. 5,000 paratroops were rushed from Belgium to save their nationals on 10 July. On the following day Katanga, whose wealth was vital to the rest of the Congo, seceded from the Congolese Republic and welcomed the Belgian intervention. Many neutrals considered this to be an attempt by Belgium to keep Katangese wealth for herself and her immensely powerful company, the *Union Minière*. Khrushchev immediately offered Soviet aid to the Congo to preserve her independence against Western aggression. America replied that she would tolerate no military forces in the Congo save those invited by the United Nations. Authority had vanished and as in Germany and elsewhere the forces of the Cold War seemed likely to be drawn into the vacuum.

The new Congolese government was divided among itself. Its President, Joseph Kasavubu, wished to set up a loose federation of self-governing tribal areas in the Congo. In this he was supported by the Katangese leader, Tshombe, who wished to use Katanga's wealth for her own benefit and not that of the poorer northern and eastern areas and the central government at Leopoldville. The nationalist leader and Prime Minister, Patrice Lumumba, a former tax and postal clerk upon whom grave responsibilities had been thrust, wanted a strong united state with a powerful central government. In desperation he appealed for a U.N. force to preserve order. By mid-July such

83   September 1960. Mobutu's soldiers manhandle Patrice Lumumba, the Congolese Prime Minister, after his arrest

84   November 1964. White mercenaries attack a house at Kindu in the Congo during a drive against pro-Lumumba rebels

order as existed was being preserved by this force and the Belgians. Kasavubu and Lumumba each announced the deposition of the other and while the West supported Kasavubu, Russia began to send Lumumba planes and lorries for troop transport. Swarms of Russian technicians and agents poured into the Congo, and Russia declared its readiness to support the Lumumba régime with volunteers and Russian regular forces. When Lumumba demanded that the U.N. forces be used to eject the Belgians and recapture Katanga the U.N. refused. Khrushchev, however, had backed the wrong side. In September Lumumba was deposed and arrested by Colonel Mobutu, the commander of the Congolese army, who on 16 September 1960 expelled the Russian embassy, machines, and technicians from the Congo. Lumumba, who was murdered with Tshombe's complicity in February 1961, became a world martyr for Communists and anti-imperialists and an African university in Moscow was named after him. His supporters, aided this time by Communist China, rebelled in 1964 and for a time controlled a number of the Congo's eastern provinces, but after the Russian expulsion the chance of Communist success in the Congo was lost. During the next six years a semblance of order was tortuously restored to a Congolese Republic with which Katanga was eventually reunited.

It seemed that world communism might receive some compensation when the left-wing Afro-Shirazi Party overthrew with much bloodshed the Sultan of Zanzibar and the ruling National Party in June 1964. Both Russia and China rushed to aid and acclaim the new government, but fears of Communist infiltration of Africa from Zanzibar were unrealised and the island merged with Tanganyika to form the state of Tanzania three months later.

Khrushchev could not afford such a humiliating failure as he had suffered in the Congo, which was to drive him to adopt more reckless courses in the future.

85   Moise Tshombe, the Katangese leader, argues with U.N. Ethiopian troops after being refused passage at a road-block

11 Crisis over Berlin

WHEN MOLOTOV ANNOUNCED to the Supreme Soviet in February 1955 that Russia had 'made such progress in the manufacture of nuclear weapons that . . . the U.S.A. is lagging behind . . .', his statement had been regarded as Soviet propaganda. Khrushchev's nuclear threat during the Suez crisis was similarly dismissed. Then on 14 October 1957 the Russians put a Sputnik, a satellite containing instruments weighing 184 lb., into orbit around the earth. The scientific achievement was tremendous but the military implications were grave. Both sides were experimenting with inter-continental missiles capable of travelling 6,000 to 9,000 miles. A rocket that could put this satellite into orbit could carry a nuclear warhead accurately to any target in America. A month later, when Russia put a second satellite into orbit carrying a dog, panic spread throughout the United States. Russia was undoubtedly ahead in the race to produce accurate inter-continental ballistic missiles (I.C.B.M.s), which could not be prevented from reaching their targets. The U.S.A. would have for some time only bombers, which could be destroyed, and medium- or intermediate-range missiles sited either on ships or in allied countries which could be blackmailed by the Russian nuclear threats into surrender. Dismayed experts forecast that the West would be faced from about 1961 with a 'missile gap', a period when Russia would have a decisive nuclear superiority and might be tempted to destroy America with one single blow.

American air force and missile bases were known to Russia and could be destroyed before retaliation could take place. Missile-carrying aircraft-carriers and submarines could be tracked. Even when American I.C.B.M.s were ready they could be destroyed by surprise attack. Their fuel was liquid oxygen which had to be loaded immediately before firing. The delay involved could be fatal. Not until the mid-1960s was it estimated that America would have land-based, solid-fuel, Minuteman I.C.B.M.s sited underground, and Polaris intermediate-range missiles which could be fired underwater from undetectable nuclear submarines. Only then would the 'gap' be closed and America have a satisfactory deterrent from nuclear attack. By this time, however, America might no longer exist. As frightened Americans began to build deep 'fall out' shelters to protect them from radiation the world entered a period described by one expert as 'the delicate balance of terror'. Each side had weapons with which it could destroy the other. Victory would lie with the side that struck first and destroyed the other's weapons. Here the advantage lay decidedly with Russia, which now tried to break out of the military encirclement which America had painstakingly created around her.

At the moment that Russia seemed to have gained superiority Khrushchev emerged from the Kremlin power struggle as supreme leader. The fact that Russia was no longer threatened with imminent nuclear destruction as it had been for the past 12 years gave him additional confidence. He had already been severely criticised by tougher Russian leaders for his handling of the Eastern European satellites, while Communist China was growing increasingly critical of the process of de-Stalinisation. Stalin had successfully built up Russia's great European empire. To prove himself a worthy successor Khrushchev had to succeed where Stalin had failed – in Yugoslavia and Berlin.

A reconciliation with Tito was effected when Khrushchev flew to Yugoslavia in May 1955, but the task of driving the West from Berlin was much more difficult.

West Berlin had long been a 'bone in the throat' for Ulbricht and Russia, threatening Russian control of East Germany and therefore of her satellite empire. Since 1949 America and West Germany had poured money into it to make it a shop-window for the West in contrast to the grim austerity of East Germany. It had also become the escape route for thousands of East Germans who slipped into the Western zone and were then flown out to West Germany. Between 1949 and 1958 2,188,000 East Germans of a total population of 17½ million had escaped through this 'hole in the Iron Curtain' which the East German *Volkspolizei* were unable to seal. Many of the escapees were farmers or had technical and professional qualifications. Their disappearance had a serious economic effect upon East Germany. The Western refusal to recognise Ulbricht's government had left West Berlin a dangerously exposed outpost in hostile territory, and in November 1958 Khrushchev announced that the time had come for all occupying powers to leave Berlin which should be handed to East Germany. If no agreement was reached on this matter by 27 May 1959 he threatened to hand the Western access routes to Berlin to East Germany. If the West attempted to use these routes without East German consent East Germany would have full Soviet support. America, Britain, and France could either withdraw or fight Russia in a nuclear war. A series of threats culminated on Christmas Day 1958 in a statement by the Soviet Foreign Minister, Gromyko, that 'any provocation in Berlin' could begin 'a big war in . . . which millions upon millions would perish . . . and the flames of war would reach the American continent. . . .'

The Russian ultimatum spread consternation throughout the West. If West Berlin was abandoned then America's other NATO allies, feeling she could no longer protect them, would withdraw from the American alliance and capitulate to Russia, thus breaking the American circle of containment. In Britain, a certain target for Russian attack since she possessed her own nuclear weapons, a strong Campaign for Nuclear Disarmament called for the abandonment of both nuclear arms and the American alliance. While the Western governments stood firm and declared their intention to remain in Berlin many people inevitably asked themselves: 'Why die in a radioactive desert for Berlin?'

As the war of nerves continued Khrushchev showed some inclination to recoil from

86   September 1959. Khrushchev visits New York. *Front row from left*: Mrs Nina Khrushchev, Gromyko (Russian Foreign Minister), Khrushchev, Hammarskjöld (U.N. Secretary-General), Kuznetsov (Russian Ambassador)

87   Moscow, August 1960. Gary Powers, the captured U.S. pilot, on trial. In front, before microphones, his Russian Defence Counsel

a final confrontation. The date of the transfer of power to East Germany was put back. Between May and July the Foreign Ministers negotiated fruitlessly at Geneva, but on 3 August an announcement was made that Khrushchev and Eisenhower would exchange friendship visits, and immediately the tension eased. On 15 September Khrushchev, his family, and entourage arrived in Washington. During a whirlwind tour of America he terrified security officials by mixing with the crowds. In a sensational address to the United Nations in New York he proposed complete disarmament within four years and after three days of informal discussion with President Eisenhower at Camp David left America declaring the Cold War to be virtually over. A Summit Conference was fixed for 16 May 1960 in Paris to discuss the main problems affecting world peace.

For a brief moment the world wondered if indeed a true reconciliation might be near but already in both camps harsher councils were beginning to prevail. John Foster Dulles, the uncompromising American Secretary of State who had directed American foreign policy since 1952, had resigned through mortal illness in April 1959. Eisenhower, who was a soldier rather than a politician, had come under the influence of more moderate advisers who urged him to explore all avenues to avert nuclear war. When Khrushchev left he believed he had secured some concessions, but American State Department officials hastened to repair the damage. Their efforts were aided by visits to America from West German Chancellor Adenauer and the French President de Gaulle in March and April 1960. These emphasised that there should be no concessions or negotiations over Berlin. Similarly Khrushchev's unorthodox methods and growing list of failures were critically viewed not only by tougher Communist leaders in Moscow but also by the Chinese, with whom relations were growing more strained. To maintain his own position Khrushchev had to secure some concessions at the Summit Meeting. If he did not there was a grave danger that he would try to restore his tarnished prestige by violent action in Berlin.

The Summit, however, was not to be. Since 1956 America had been secretly sending high-flying U2 reconnaissance planes over Russia to photograph military installations. On 5 May 1960, eleven days before the Summit was due to take place, Khrushchev announced that a U2 had been shot down 1,200 miles inside Soviet territory near Sverdlovsk. It had been flying from a base in Pakistan to Norway (see Map 8). When the Americans denied a charge of espionage Khrushchev produced the captured pilot and his equipment, thus humiliating America before world opinion. Eisenhower then justified the flights and on the day before the Summit placed American forces on alert throughout the world. At the first meeting of the Summit Khrushchev

88   The Berlin Wall. West Berlin police try to bring over the body of an East German, shot by the *Volkspolizei*

89   U.S. tanks (*foreground*) face Soviet tanks at Checkpoint Charlie

demanded an apology for the incident. When Eisenhower refused, the Summit dissolved in confusion without having begun. Berlin was temporarily forgotten and Khrushchev's prestige was saved. Many also condemned American irresponsibility in sending U2 aircraft over Russia at this or indeed at any time, since they could be considered to be carrying nuclear bombs and thus provoke Russian nuclear retaliation. It seemed to them that America had deliberately destroyed all prospect of the Summit's success.

The Summit's failure, however, provided Khrushchev with only a temporary respite. With Chinese and domestic pressure increasing, to survive as Russian ruler he had to drive the West from Berlin. A meeting with the new American President Kennedy in Vienna on 3–4 June 1961 brought no prospect of an easy victory. When Khrushchev repeated his ultimatum and again threatened a separate peace treaty with East Germany, which would isolate West Berlin, tension again mounted. On 8 July Russian defence expenditure was increased by a third. A fortnight later Kennedy called for a corresponding increase in NATO and American forces. Flights from East Berlin rose to 20,000 a month as many took what they believed was their last chance to escape. Then on 13 August, East German police, jeered by thousands of West Berliners, and guarded by tanks and armoured cars, sealed off West Berlin except for a number of official crossing points. This was followed on the night of 17–18 August by the erection of a 6-foot concrete wall surmounted with barbed wire which divided the city in two. West Berliners were no longer allowed to enter the Eastern zone without special visas.

Western troops patrolled up to the wall with tanks, armoured cars, and anti-tank guns, and when American Vice-President Johnson visited the city on 19 August he deliberately drove into East Berlin. General Clay, Kennedy's special envoy to Berlin, also purposely sent American troops into the Eastern sector to demonstrate their right of access, and American tanks took up position at the Friedrichstrasse crossing point. The day after Johnson's visit 1,500 American reinforcements and 250 tanks arrived in Berlin, and on 25 August a call-up of American reservists was announced. Despite this show of force everyone knew that the 11,000 allied troops in Berlin were no more than a 'trip wire', since the Russians and East Germans could muster 67,000 troops and 1,200 tanks within 30 miles. If a clash came the final verdict would rest with nuclear weapons.

Since November 1958 America, Britain, and Russia had suspended nuclear tests, but on 21 August testing was resumed in Russia and by 30 October the Russians had produced over 50 nuclear explosions intended to intimidate the West. The last one of over 50 megatons, the equivalent of 50 million tons of T.N.T., was the greatest explosion then recorded. By 1961, however, the deep despondency created by the 'missile gap' was passing and America had regained much confidence in her nuclear strength. Intelligence sources considered that Russia had not been able to manufacture the number of bombs which she was thought capable of making in 1955. America still had a great superiority in long-range bombers and since 1959 had been busily installing medium-range and intermediate-range ballistic missiles in Britain, Italy, and Turkey. She also had operational Polaris submarines with missiles travelling 1,500 miles which could bombard Russia from the Mediterranean, Baltic, Arctic, or Pacific (see Map 8).

The Berlin Wall had stopped the drain of manpower to the West, although it was hardly a good advertisement for communism, particularly when escapees were shot and left to die. Khrushchev now sought for a Russian missile base in the Western Hemisphere which would lay America open to local attack and leave him in a position to dictate terms upon Berlin and possibly much else.

101

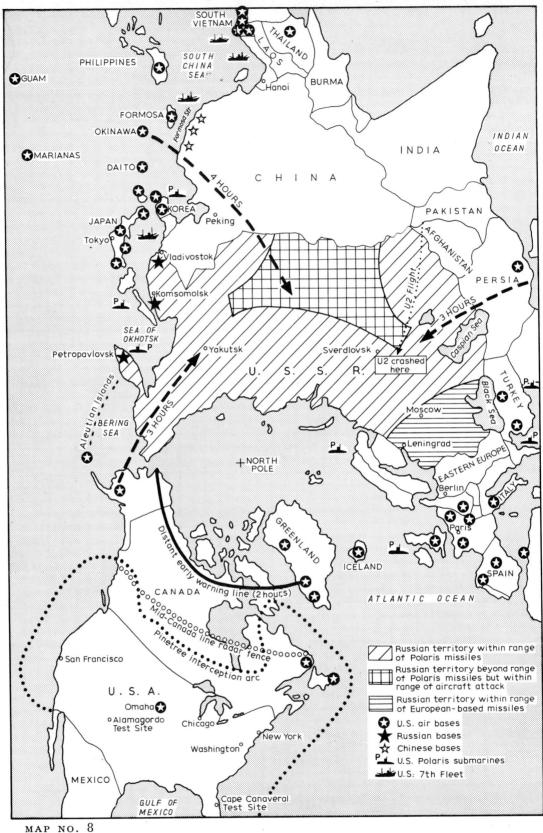

PHILIPPINES

GUAM

SOUTH VIETNAM

THAILAND

LAOS

BURMA

SOUTH CHINA SEA

Hanoi

INDIA

INDIAN OCEAN

FORMOSA

OKINAWA

MARIANAS

DAITO

Formosa Str.

CHINA

PAKISTAN

AFGHANISTAN

4 HOURS

KOREA

Peking

JAPAN

Tokyo

Vladivostok

PERSIA

U2 Flight

3 HOURS

Komsomolsk

SEA OF OKHOTSK

Yakutsk

Sverdlovsk

U2 crashed here

Caspian Sea

U. S. S. R.

Petropavlovsk

Aleutian Islands

BERING SEA

3 HOURS

Moscow

Black Sea

TURKEY

Leningrad

NORTH POLE

EASTERN EUROPE

Berlin

ITALY

Distant early warning line (2 hours)

GREENLAND

Paris

Mid-Canada line radar fence

CANADA

Pinetree interception arc

ICELAND

SPAIN

ATLANTIC OCEAN

San Francisco

U. S. A.

Omaha

Alamagordo Test Site

Chicago

New York

Russian territory within range of Polaris missiles

Russian territory beyond range of Polaris missiles but within range of aircraft attack

Russian territory within range of European-based missiles

★ U.S. air bases
★ Russian bases
☆ Chinese bases
P U.S. Polaris submarines
U.S. 7th Fleet

Washington

MEXICO

GULF OF MEXICO

Cape Canaveral Test Site

MAP NO. 8
THE AMERICAN CONTAINMENT OF COMMUNISM

12 Confrontation in Cuba

CENTRAL AND SOUTH AMERICA had long possessed the corrupt governments, extremes in wealth and poverty, and tendencies towards popular revolt which encourage the spread of communism. In the immediate post-war years communism had gained ground especially in Colombia, where in 1948 a Pan-American Conference at Bogotá was delayed for several days by Communist riots. It emerged next in British Guiana, a colony on the north-east coast of South America, where a constitution was granted in 1953 (see Map 9). In the general election which followed in April 1953 the People's Progressive Party (PPP) led by Cheddi Jagan was overwhelmingly successful, winning 18 of the 24 seats. With a crowded population on a narrow sea coast, housing, health, and social conditions were extremely poor. The PPP had been elected with Jagan as Prime Minister upon a programme of land reform and the nationalisation of industry. Once in power it also began to demand internal self-government and the abolition of the reserved powers of the Governor. After widespread strikes of sugar-workers through-out September the British Colonial Office on 6 October accused Jagan of attempting to establish a Communist régime. The constitution was suspended and British naval and military forces were despatched to Georgetown. When the PPP members were relieved of their government posts a general strike was called. This was unsuccessful, but wide-spread sugar strikes throughout November were accompanied by sabotage and arson, and eventually most of the PPP leaders were arrested.

Trouble occurred next in Guatemala where Communist influence had been growing in the labour movement since the revolution of 1944. In March 1951 Arbenz Guzman was elected President with Communist support. After his election Communist influence in the government steadily increased. The Communist Party functioned openly. Its members held key government posts, land redistribution began, and

90 22 October 1962. President John F. Kennedy makes his momentous speech in which he announces the U.S. blockade of Cuba

MAP NO. 9   THE CUBAN CRISIS (1962)

internal opposition was crushed. Guatemala's left-wing policies soon caused tensions with her neighbours. In February 1953 the plantations of the great American United Fruit Company were confiscated and given to landless peasants. The British and American-owned Central American Railway Company was also taken over. As U.S. fears of a Communist outpost on the American continent grew, neighbouring dictatorships began to fear the Guatemalan example might spread. By January 1954 Guatemala claimed that Nicaragua, El Salvador, the Dominican Republic, and Venezuela were planning to invade her with U.S. support (see Map 9). Arms and money were provided by the United Fruit Company and other businessmen to a force of exiles and foreign recruits raised by the Catholic Colonel Castillo Armas, who had been exiled from Guatemala in 1951. When a large arms shipment arrived in Guatemala from Poland, the United States feared that Guatemala planned to dominate Central America. Military pacts were hurriedly made with Nicaragua and Honduras, and U.S. arms flown to them. Then on 18 June Castillo's forces supported by aircraft invaded Guatemala from Honduras. There was little fighting since the Guatemalan army officers refused to fight. Arbenz resigned on 27 June and took refuge in the Mexican embassy. The right to vote was taken from the illiterate peasantry who had elected him. The Communist Party was banned and 2,000 Communists were arrested. Communist attempts to establish a beachhead in the Western Hemisphere had again been frustrated but in the explosive conditions of Latin America it was only a matter of time before they succeeded.

Since 1952 the neighbouring Caribbean island of Cuba had been ruled by the harsh dictatorship of General Fulgencio Batista. In July 1953 Fidel Castro, a young lawyer and champion of the poor, attempted with his brother Raúl and a band of 160 supporters to overthrow Batista's police state. Their attack on the army barracks at Santiago de Cuba on 26 July 1953 failed disastrously. Half the rebels were killed and Castro after a term of imprisonment went into exile.

In December 1956 he returned. 82 members of the '26th of July Movement' landed on the coast of Oriente province. Batista's forces, however, were awaiting them and only twelve, including Castro, escaped to the hills of the Sierra Maestra range. Here they established a guerrilla force which was soon 5,000 strong with many sympathisers in Havana and the cities. Attacks on government troops, communications, and plantations provoked brutal retaliation from Batista, who drove more and more people to Castro's side. A rising in Havana in April 1958 was crushed after bitter street fighting, but by the autumn of 1958 Castro felt strong enough to come into the open and fight a conventional war. Six guerrilla columns began a westward march to liberate Cuba. By December they controlled half the island. On 23 December Batista launched a counter-offensive supported by planes and tanks, and a fierce battle ensued around the town of Santa Clara. After hard fighting the rebels won. Many of Batista's troops deserted to Castro. Guerrilla supporters of Castro emerged in Batista's own areas and the Batista régime collapsed. The dictator took refuge in the Dominican Republic and many of his supporters fled to the U.S.A. As hundreds of political prisoners were freed Castro and his guerrillas, fêted by vast crowds, triumphantly entered Havana on 8 January 1959. Officials of the hated Batista régime were tried and executed on the spot, and widespread measures were passed to wipe out the graft and corruption which had been a part of Cuban life.

Castro at first denied allegations of communism and any personal political ambitions except the re-establishment of democracy. By 16 February, however, he had become Prime Minister and a programme of land reform began, involving the confiscation of American sugar mills and plantations. Between June and August 1959 small bands of exiles unsuccessfully attempted the invasion of the Dominican Republic, Nicaragua, Panama, and Haiti. These attempts to copy the pattern of the Cuban revolution, often with Cuban support, again aroused American fears. As government control over the Cuban economy increased and the confiscation of foreign property continued, the relationship between Cuba and the United States deteriorated. Acts of sabotage and attempts to bomb the sugar crop by Batistan exiles in private planes from Florida made matters worse. One-third of Cuba's national income came from her sugar crop and 50,000 militia were recruited to guard it since without it Cuba would be ruined.

In May 1960 America announced the end of economic aid to Cuba and two months later cut her imports of Cuban sugar. She was too late. Russia had already offered Cuba machinery and technical assistance, and arranged to buy sugar. Supplies of Russian crude oil followed plus further technical agreements with Poland, Czechoslovakia, and East Germany. When U.S., British, and Dutch refineries in Cuba refused to refine the Russian oil they were nationalised. The Cuban sugar which the U.S. had refused was also bought by Moscow. Threatened by the fate of Guatemala Cuba had obtained the protection of what the jubilant Castro described as 'the most powerful nation in the world'. Khrushchev was quick to seize his chance and threaten retaliation against U.S. intervention in Cuba, with Russian rockets that Pacific tests had just

91   Cheddi Jagan, leader of the PPP in
British Guiana

92   January 1959. Fidel Castro enters
Havana in triumph

proved would travel 8,000 miles. The Cold War had entered the Caribbean and
tension grew. Two further attempts at armed rebellion encouraged by the United
States were crushed in Cuba in October 1960. Cuban-inspired risings in Nicaragua
and Guatemala were equally unsuccessful the following month. As Castro turned
increasingly towards communism many of his early supporters fled to Florida and their
places were taken by known Communists. Large quantities of arms arrived from the
Soviet bloc to supply Castro's 40,000 regulars and 200,000 militiamen who made up the
largest army in Latin America.

U.S. diplomatic relations with Cuba were broken off on 3 January 1961. Unable
to take direct action against Cuba without arousing the opposition of Latin America
and much of the world, the U.S.A. began to train an army of Cuban exiles in the hope
that their invasion might turn discontent with the Castro régime into revolution. On
17 April 1961 this force landed from America at the Bay of Pigs in south Cuba (see Map
9). The attempt was a complete disaster for America. Castro's militia did not defect as
was hoped. Three days' heavy fighting resulted in complete victory for Castro who took
1,200 prisoners and destroyed the rest of the invaders.

Fearing the United States might try again, Castro looked increasingly to Russia
for help. Before the close of 1961 a Russian military mission to Cuba had been followed
by combat units of Russian troops. In the spring of 1962, as American anxiety mounted,
Russian anti-aircraft batteries were installed with ground-to-air rockets which could
shoot down U2 spy planes. Finally in September 1962 in the greatest secrecy Russian
technicians began the installation of medium- and intermediate-range ballistic missiles
in western Cuba and the assembly of Russian bombers, transported in crates to Cuba,
which were capable of carrying nuclear bombs. Castro's aim was undoubtedly defensive
but on 18 October Russia's Foreign Minister, Gromyko, had informed President
Kennedy that Russia intended to make a separate peace with Germany on 6 November,
which would bring the long-smouldering Berlin issue to a head. By this time the rockets
would be ready, pointing at the heart of America. Once operational they could not be
dismantled without the risk of being fired. On 14 October a U2 flying over Cuba took
photographs which when developed the following day launched the world into the

gravest crisis of its history. These and subsequent photographs revealed that the Russians were installing no less than ten missile bases 90 miles from the American coast. The medium-range missiles with a range of 1,200 miles were capable of striking Washington, the Panama Canal, or the U.S. Atlantic Missile Range at Cape Canaveral in Florida. The intermediate-range missiles travelling 2,000 miles could be launched upon any of the major cities of the Western Hemisphere (see Map 9). Experts estimated that the rockets would be operational by November, so that there was no time to lose.

After a week of frenzied secret preparation an American air and land attack upon Cuba using conventional weapons was scheduled to begin at dawn on 30 October if no agreement could be reached. In a dramatic television broadcast to America on the evening of 22 October President Kennedy revealed the full gravity of the crisis. He announced a naval blockade of Cuba to prevent the delivery of further military equipment and instructed the U.S. armed forces to prepare for all eventualities.

Reinforcements were despatched to the American base at Guantanamo in eastern Cuba and a resolution tabled at the United Nations calling for the dismantling and withdrawal of the Russian missiles before the blockade would be lifted. Any nuclear missiles launched from Cuba against any nation in the Western Hemisphere would be treated, warned Kennedy, as an attack by Russia upon the United States and would bring instant retaliation upon the Soviet Union.

> We will not [he stated] . . . unnecessarily risk the cost of world wide nuclear war in which even the fruits of victory would be ashes in our mouth but neither will we shrink from that risk at any time it must be faced. . . .[1]

A note delivered to Russia demanding the withdrawal of the missiles warned that she had little time to decide. Aware that an attack could be made upon Berlin while attention was centred upon Cuba American nuclear forces were put in readiness throughout the world. All leave was cancelled for the Soviet forces and the forces of the Warsaw Pact countries mobilised. In Cuba Castro's militia prepared to resist invasion. After 17 years of gathering tension the two super-powers had reached the brink of war.

By 24 October Cuba was ringed with U.S. aircraft-carriers, cruisers, and destroyers while 25 Communist-bloc ships sailed towards the island. As troops, marines, and aircraft gathered in southern Florida construction of the missile bases feverishly continued. In the United Nations 40 neutral countries tried desperately to find some compromise which would save the world from destruction. The discovery of Khrushchev's scheme had, however, placed him in an extremely difficult position. He could not stand by and watch the Russian troops in Cuba overwhelmed by an American invasion. Cuba was too distant to be given conventional help and the Russians lacked command of the sea. His only alternative was nuclear war.

On the night of 24 October the 12 Russian ships carrying military equipment turned back. On 27 October Khrushchev offered to remove the Russian bases from Cuba if the U.S.A. would dismantle her rocket bases in Turkey. When this offer was ignored he finally agreed on 28 October to dismantle and withdraw the missiles in return for an American pledge not to invade Cuba. The world, which had been two days from disaster, breathed again. The pledge to Cuba enabled Khrushchev to save

[1] Keesing's Contemporary Archives, p. 19060.

93   An air-photograph showing a Russian ground-to-air
missile installation in Cuba

face somewhat but there was no separate Russian peace treaty with East Germany and
no further attempt to drive the allies from Berlin.

The Cuban crisis was a turning point in the Cold War. It had a sobering effect
upon Russia and the West who had both come so close to nuclear devastation. Within
a year a Partial Test Ban Treaty had been signed in Moscow on 5 August 1963 by
America, Russia, Britain, and many other powers, banning all nuclear tests on land,
sea, or in the air. A 'hot line' was also installed for direct communication between the
Kremlin and the White House which would make last-minute contact possible between
the leaders of the super-powers to avoid disaster if such a grave crisis ever arose again.
In October 1964 Khrushchev was suddenly dismissed from his offices and Alexei
Kosygin and Leonid Brezhnev became premier and First Secretary respectively. Theirs
was a much more sober government that would avoid the dangerous risks that Khrushchev had taken. Henceforth the Cold War contestants would maintain a verbal battle,
still seeking to secure advantage over each other when world circumstances offered,
but avoiding a major confrontation such as Cuba. Both, too, were increasingly influenced by a common fear of Communist China, who had not signed the Partial Test Ban
Treaty and in October 1964 had exploded her first atomic bomb.

13 The Sino-Soviet Split

AFTER THE CHINESE COMMUNIST VICTORY of 1949 Mao had hoped for Russian aid to build a modern industrial Communist state. At first this seemed likely and the Sino-Soviet military alliance of February 1950 was followed by generous Russian financial and technical help.

Although to some extent protected by the Russian alliance Mao nevertheless took a tremendous risk when he entered the Korean war. He challenged not only 16 countries of the United Nations but also the United States which had crushed Japan in World War II. Had the U.S. turned her nuclear might against him as many Americans had urged, his newly founded People's Republic could have been destroyed and Chiang Kai-Shek returned to power. His success in the Korean war only strengthened his view that Russian power was great and that the Western powers were 'paper tigers' whom there was no need to fear. Since 1927 he and the other Chinese Communist leaders had known nothing but war. They therefore came quickly to believe that peace could only result from a final military victory of world communism. Chinese communism therefore became tougher in its outlook than that of Russia itself.

Friendly relations between Russia and China nevertheless continued until 1956 when Khrushchev's sudden denial of Stalin plunged the Communist world everywhere into confusion. Although Stalin had given little assistance to Mao during his struggle with Chiang, Mao had nevertheless regarded him as the world leader of 'tough' communism. None of the other world Communist parties had been consulted before the denunciation and the Chinese were disturbed. The upheavals in Poland and Hungary which followed de-Stalinisation added to their disquiet, especially when these were accompanied by Russian attempts at a *détente*. Nevertheless, although puzzled, China still continued to recognise Russian leadership of world communism since she was the strongest military and economic power.

After 1950 America was even more China's enemy than Russia's. While Russia had also to consider Britain, France, and West Germany, the European colonial powers were fast withdrawing from the Far East where only India could possibly rival China. America, however, was a constant stumbling block to Chinese Far Eastern ambitions. She had not only her great naval and air base at Okinawa but also bases in and alliances with Japan, the Philippines, Thailand, and South Korea. Worse still, she had given protection to South Vietnam and Chiang's islands of Formosa, Quemoy, and Matsu. After the Korean war the U.S. 7th Fleet, equipped with nuclear weapons, patrolled the Formosa Straits (see Map 8). China with no navy was powerless to challenge it. In 1955 America had concluded a treaty with Chiang Kai-Shek, and while he remained free to attack the Chinese mainland, Dulles warned that any Communist action in the Far East would be met by 'massive retaliation'.

Until the autumn of 1957 Mao's hands were tied. Then with the dramatic news of Russia's nuclear superiority his moment seemed to have come. Communism was at last stronger than the West. Russian missiles could be used to take Formosa, and America dared not resist. With Russian weapons and China's manpower the triumph of world communism could not be stopped.

The Russians, however, were disappointingly slow to use their newly-acquired supremacy in a final confrontation. When American troops landed in the Lebanon

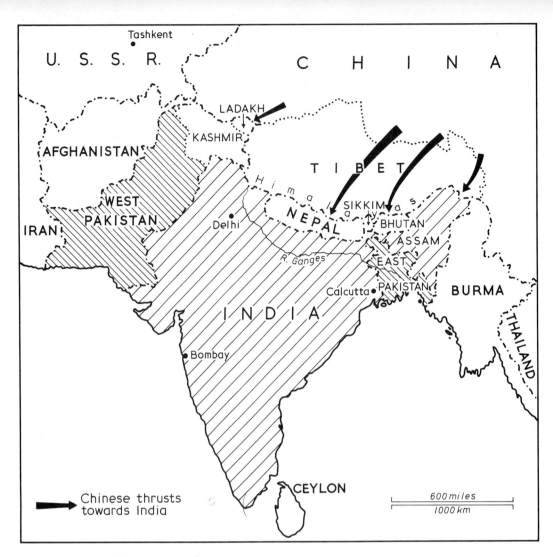

in July 1958 China immediately promised 'People's Volunteers' but there was no corresponding Russian response. To goad the Russians to action Mao began an artillery and aerial bombardment of Quemoy on 23 August. The Nationalists held their ground. Their American fighters with air-to-air missiles proved superior to the Communist planes. On 4 September Dulles threatened to bomb the batteries on the Chinese mainland, and after talks the bombardment stopped. During the crisis the Russians were non-committal. Only when it was over did they begin to offer aid, and Mao's disillusion grew.

During the next two years the rift widened as Khrushchev's 'soft' policies increasingly appeared to represent a betrayal of communism. When his Berlin ultimatum came to naught the Chinese were openly critical. When he flew to the tenth anniversary celebrations of the People's Republic in September 1959 after his Camp David meetings with Eisenhower, he received a very cool reception. Next month, after the flight of the Dalai Lama from Tibet, a border clash occurred between China and India. Chinese maps already ominously showed 32,000 square miles of Indian territory in Ladakh, Sikkim, Bhutan, and Nepal as belonging to China (see Map 10). When a patrol of Indian policemen was overwhelmed 40 miles inside the Ladakh border by Chinese troops Russia remained neutral. Since a visit by Khrushchev in 1955 large-scale Russian economic aid had been poured into India and the Russians were not prepared to endanger their diplomatic success by support of China. Chinese anger was increased by the feeling that the Russian aid to India should have gone to themselves.

By 1956 most of China's land had been grouped into large collective farms. When these failed to produce sufficient food, and industrial production remained low, Mao in 1958 had introduced a drastic re-organisation of Chinese life by a 'Great Leap Forward'. The entire population had been grouped into huge 'communes' of 60,000 to 80,000 people who lived and worked together in agriculture and industry and organised their own free housing, education, health services, militia, food and clothing. The communes were intended not only to create a classless society, where all served the community and lived and were paid equally together, but also to free women from family cares to swell the labour force, and to transfer many workers from farming to industry. The 'Leap Forward', however, was almost a disaster. Food production slumped and famine was narrowly avoided. Within three years many communes were replaced by the earlier village units. The Chinese, therefore, with some justification felt that they had more right to Russian help than non-Communist India.

The quarrel culminated in 1960. After increasing Chinese criticism of Khrushchev's agreement to the Summit talks there were angry exchanges between Khrushchev and Chinese delegates at the summer congress of the Romanian Communist Party. The Chinese claimed that the Russian fear of war had led her to abandon true communism whose leadership had now passed to China. The army of Russian technicians who had been helping the development of Chinese industry were suddenly recalled, taking with them even the plans of the factories they had been building. An agreement to aid China in the production of the atomic bomb was torn up. Russia and China shared an ill-defined frontier of 4,500 miles (see Map 4). China had the largest and one of the most hungry populations in the world. Russia had much empty land. The two powers had old frontier disputes and the questions of the status of Inner Mongolia and Manchuria to settle. In the nineteenth century Russia had seized much Chinese territory, and the Russians had a traditional fear of the Asiatic hordes who had ravaged their lands in the Middle Ages. A China which was not subservient was feared and could not be tolerated. From June 1960 the verbal struggle grew more violent, Russia found a new Cold War on its hands, and the world Communist camp was hopelessly split. While the Asian and African Communist parties supported China, the European parties, except Albania, beyond reach of the Soviet armies, supported Russia. The fact that it had to compete for their support again weakened Russia's hold over the East European satellites and enabled countries like Romania to assert more independence in the 1960s.

Mao Tse-Tung had never disguised the fact that he believed China, with its immense population, could survive the effects of a nuclear war. Over Cuba Russia showed unmistakably that it was prepared to take no such risk to secure world communism, and in subsequent international crises acted in closer concert with the West to pacify world trouble-spots before a clash could arise. Throughout 1962 Sino-Indian relations deteriorated until in October–November they reached a state of undeclared war. On 20 October in the midst of the Cuban crisis over which the Chinese ridiculed

94 A wounded Indian soldier is rushed
to a helicopter during border fighting
against the Chinese in the North-East
Frontier area

95 Tashkent, January 1966. President
Ayub Khan of Pakistan shakes hands
with Lal Bahadur Shastri, Indian Prime
Minister (*left*), and Kosygin

the Russians, Chinese armies launched a major offensive against Ladakh and the
North-East Frontier area (see Map 10). Overwhelmed, the Indian army fell back. While
Russia remained neutral British and American arms were rushed to India's aid, but by
mid-November Ladakh was lost and the Chinese were within 30 miles of the fertile
plains of Assam. Then suddenly on 21 November the Chinese announced a cease-fire
and withdrew behind the lines they had occupied in November 1959. Diplomats
wondered if this sudden change had been caused by pressure from Russia and the offer
of Russian aid to India.

The complex situation in India, however, remained unsettled. Western aid to
India alarmed India's Moslem neighbour, Pakistan, who feared the weapons might be
used against her. Despite Western pressure to unite with India against the common
enemy, Pakistan came to an agreement with China in July 1963. Since the partition of
India in 1947 India and Pakistan had disputed over the province of Kashmir. When
open war broke out in the autumn of 1965 and fighting began in Kashmir and the
Punjab plains, Russia was undoubtedly pleased at America's embarrassment since the
arms she had been pouring into India to contain China were now turned against her
CENTO and SEATO ally Pakistan, who had China's full support. On 17 September,
however, China entered the dispute with an ultimatum to India to demolish defences
on the Tibetan border with Sikkim. Chinese troops massed along the Himalayan frontier
and India was forced to keep a large part of her army facing these instead of fighting
Pakistan.

With the threat of a Chinese invasion of India, Russia and America hastily combined to stop the war. Russia played a prominent part in securing a cease-fire which
came into operation on 22 September 1965, and on 10 January 1966 Mr Kosygin
persuaded India and Pakistan to sign a peace agreement at Tashkent in which they
foreswore war as a means of settlement in Kashmir. This was the first occasion that the
super-powers had acted together since the founding of the United Nations, and the
American Secretary of State, Dean Rusk, went so far as to praise Russia for 'her helpful
attitude', in the crisis.

When the Middle East erupted into the Five-Day Arab-Israeli war on 5 June 1967
the same restraint by Russia and America was evident. Since 1956 there had been
constant border clashes between Israel and her Arab neighbours, Syria, Egypt, and

96   Jerusalem, June 1967. Israeli
soldiers in the captured Jordanian sector
of the city

97 Russian naval officers of the Soviet
cruiser *October Revolution* at Port Said.
After the June War Russia gained a
Mediterranean foothold

Jordan, who were still united only in their intention of destroying the 3 million Jews. By
1967 Syria, which had a Marxist government, and Nasser's Egypt had been heavily
armed with modern planes and equipment by Russia while Israel remained the only
reliable bastion of Western influence in the Middle East. In May Nasser dismissed the
U.N. force which had patrolled the Egyptian-Israeli border since 1956 and massed his
armies in the Sinai Desert and the Gaza Strip. He also again closed the Gulf of Aqaba
to Israeli shipping, thus closing the port of Eilat and Israeli access to Africa and Asia.
Egyptian warnings were issued to Britain and America that any interference would
cause the closure of the Suez Canal, a total disruption of oil supplies, and a boycott of
Western economic interests. Russia, Nasser claimed, would intervene on his behalf to
prevent a repetition of 1956. As the U.S. 6th Fleet, based on Spain, hastened to the
eastern Mediterranean, a Russian fleet moved into the area from the Bosphorus. With
the fear that Egypt might become another Cuba the danger of a great-power conflict
grew.

Neither Russia nor America was able to restrain their protégés as they would
have liked. On 5 June Israel, a tiny country that could not hope to fight a defensive
war, forestalled an Arab invasion with a *blitzkrieg* which in five days secured one of the
most decisive military victories of the twentieth century. In a few hours the combined
air forces of Syria, Jordan, and Egypt were destroyed on the ground. Guessing that the
Arabs had no unified command, the Israelis, with complete air control, then concentrated first upon Egypt and Jordan. While one force seized the Old City of Jerusalem
and overwhelmed the west bank of the Jordan, paratroops took Sharm el-Sheik, whose
guns had closed the Gulf of Aqaba. Meanwhile the main body of Israeli armour raced
southwards towards Egypt. The Israelis had some 600 tanks to Egypt's thousand, but
on the first day they cut off the Gaza Strip and while one column raced along the coast-
road to Qantara, others struck further south towards Ismailia and Taufiq. The Sinai
Desert became a vast graveyard as it witnessed the biggest tank battle in history. 700
Soviet-built tanks were captured or destroyed as two Egyptian armoured divisions and
100,000 infantry disintegrated before Israeli ground and air attack. Thousands of
Egyptian soldiers were left wandering through the waterless desert, and on 8 June the
Israelis reached the Suez Canal. The Egyptian army in Sinai was cut off and annihi-
lated. By this time Israeli contingents from Jordan had swung into Syria, which had

played little part in the hostilities. The heights from which Syria had for 19 years attacked Israel's frontier farms were taken and the war was won (see Map 7).

The tensest moment had come when Nasser and King Hussein of Jordan had claimed that planes from British and American aircraft-carriers in the Mediterranean had provided air cover for the Israelis in Sinai. Here was the cue for Russian intervention. If Russia failed to give aid she stood to lose face and the fruits of eleven years' diplomacy and economic and military aid. She was not, however, prepared to take the risk. Although supporting the Arabs publicly, in private she had tried to use her restraining influence. She voted instead for the cease-fire resolution at the United Nations and on 23 and 25 June Mr Kosygin, while in the United States for a U.N. Special Emergency Meeting, met President Johnson privately for talks at Glassboro, New Jersey. As a result of the war Russia had gained in the Arab states the 'warm water' ports for her fleet which she had so long sought. She immediately replaced the Soviet-made arms which had been lost by the Arabs but limited them to weapons of a defensive nature since she was as anxious for a Middle East settlement as the United States.

In contrast, China after 1962 emerged as a militant rival to Russia, intent upon encouraging Communist revolution in Africa, Asia, and Latin America to counter the 'Soviet-American intention of world domination'. In 1963–4 the Chinese Foreign Minister, Chou En-Lai, carried out a marathon tour of Africa during which he remarked upon the 'excellent revolutionary situation' there. His visit coincided with the left-wing *coup* in Zanzibar where China and Russia were soon competing for influence. Chinese economic aid went also to Algeria and other emergent nations. In the Congo it was Chinese and not Russian help which supported the Lumumbist rebels in 1964. African nationalist guerrillas penetrating into Rhodesia from Zambia in early 1968 were also supplied with Chinese arms.

In Asia the Communist Thailand Patriotic Front, a guerrilla organisation founded to drive out the Americans and overthrow the pro-American Thai government, was sponsored in January 1965 by Peking, who supported a similar movement in Burma. Towards the close of 1965 the Chinese-backed Indonesian Communist Party, the third largest in the world, eliminated Indonesia's six leading generals in a *coup* which failed. Half a million Indonesian Communists were massacred in the wave of anti-Communist and anti-Chinese feeling which followed. Between May and September 1967 riots and strikes by Chinese Communist sympathisers also produced a state of emergency in the British colony of Hongkong, and there were tense border clashes between British security forces and Chinese demonstrators.

In Latin America China was quick to support Cuban attempts to spread revolution to the corrupt mainland dictatorships with which Russia pursued a policy of establishing diplomatic and economic relations regardless of politics. Che Guevara, an Argentine-born Communist with Chinese sympathies who had commanded Castro's forces at Santa Clara, suddenly vanished from Cuba in March 1965 after returning from a tour of China, Africa, and Asian countries. It was announced that Guevara, an expert in guerrilla warfare like Mao Tse-Tung and Giap, had gone 'to continue the work of revolution'. His disappearance coincided with an outbreak of Communist revolutionary activity in South America, the 'back door' to the U.S.A. In Venezuela a pro-Castro guerrilla movement attempted to overthrow the government in April 1965. In May 20,000 U.S. troops were sent to the Dominican Republic to prevent the Communist takeover of a revolt to reinstate the freely elected government of leftist Juan Bosch, which had been overthrown by the army two years before. In the same month 25,000 Bolivian tin-miners, whose wages had been cut by half by the military government, revolted and seized control of several large tin-mines in the industrial district of La Paz. Their revolt was crushed by the army and 500 miners were killed. By the close of the year there were other guerrillas active in Colombia, Guatemala, and Peru. A Tri-Continental Conference in Havana in January 1966 established an Organisation for the Solidarity of Asia, Africa, and Latin America which received wholehearted Chinese support. In contrast, Mr Kosygin after his Glassboro talks visited Castro in June 1967 to try – unsuccessfully – to persuade him to end his support for Latin American revolutionaries.

Guevara's aim was to create so many guerrilla revolutions like the one in Vietnam that the United States could not deal with them and would be overwhelmed. He himself seems to have concentrated primarily upon Bolivia where he established contact with the miners. Secret rifle ranges were made for training in the mines and a band of miners left to join him at a guerrilla base in late 1966. In early 1967 guerrillas scored a number of local successes against the Bolivian army, but by September U.S.-trained Bolivian rangers had eliminated two guerrilla bands and in October Guevara was seized in a jungle ambush, shot after capture, and his body publicly displayed. For the time being, at any rate, there was to be no repetition of the Cuban revolution, and the United States was left free to find some solution to the problem of the containment of China in Vietnam, where the limited American-Soviet co-operation had not had the same effect as elsewhere.

98   Hongkong, May 1967. Riot police advance on a crowd of Chinese Communist sympathisers

99   The body of Che Guevara, displayed by the Bolivian army

100   Djarkarta, May 1965. A mass rally of the Indonesian Communist Party, held before the terrible measures taken to crush it

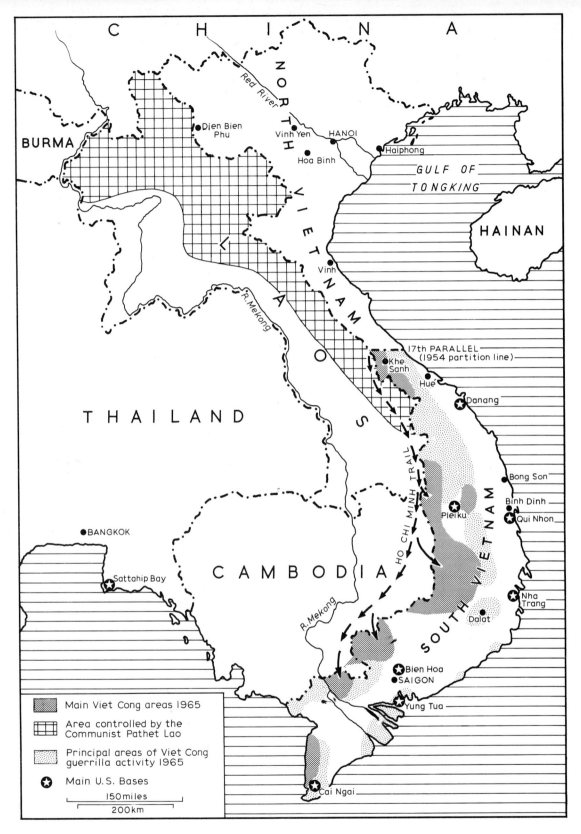

MAP NO. II VIETNAM

14 Vietnam

AFTER THE FRENCH WITHDRAWAL America had determined to cling to South Vietnam. Not only did it contain strategic naval and air bases, but if Vietnam fell then Laos and Cambodia would be next, followed closely by Thailand, Burma, and Malaya. The Americans therefore installed as President Ngo Dinh Diem, a former provincial governor, who was a dedicated Catholic and anti-Communist. 75 per cent of his government's expenditure was met by the United States, which also equipped and paid ARVN, the Army of the Republic of Vietnam. Diem's government, however, soon proved a harsh, corrupt, and inefficient family dictatorship, which introduced none of the social or land reforms necessary to win popular support. During 1957–9, as unrest with his régime grew, the former Viet Minh guerrillas reappeared in the countryside murdering government-picked headmen and local officials. When two ARVN battalions were ambushed in September 1959 near the Cambodian border the guerrilla problem blossomed into a war and America's difficulties had begun.

In December 1960 the guerrillas established a National Liberation Front of South Vietnam aiming to overthrow Diem, expel the Americans, and reunite Vietnam. Before the year was out its guerrilla army, christened the Vietcong (Vietnamese Communists) by Diem's government, was 20,000 strong and making rapid headway. ARVN had been trained to meet the danger of a formal invasion from the North and not to fight a guerrilla war. America grew alarmed and both ARVN and its military advisers were increased. At the close of 1961 there were 1,364 Americans in South Vietnam. Their number had risen to 10,000 by December 1962, and 15,500 a year later. To protect villages against terrorism and deprive the Vietcong of food, intelligence, and recruits, a 'strategic hamlet' policy began which grouped the peasants into fortified villages surrounded by barbed wire. Despite these measures the Vietcong nevertheless controlled over half the country by day and much more after dark. Supplies and reinforcements came to them from North Vietnam by the Ho Chi Minh Trail which ran through neighbouring Laos. After the Geneva agreement of 1954 the Pathet Lao Communists, aided by North Vietnam, had resisted all attempts to dislodge them from the northern forests. By May 1962, faced with the danger that communism might sweep through Laos into Cambodia and Thailand, America despatched troops to Thailand, and the other SEATO members, Britain, Australia, New Zealand, and the Philippines, followed suit.

As the crisis deepened even the Americans could no longer disregard Diem's unpopularity among his own people, and in September 1963 following his repression of the Buddhists who objected to his one-party government, America disassociated itself from his régime. Two months later he was overthrown and murdered in a military *coup*. American aid was restored but by mid-1965 a further twelve changes of government had still failed to produce a régime which would improve the condition of the people and win national support. In these chaotic political conditions Vietcong numbers by 1964 had reached 100,000. In August, in retaliation for an attack by North Vietnamese torpedo boats on U.S. destroyers in the Gulf of Tongking, American planes made their first raid upon North Vietnam, bombing naval bases and an oil storage depot. American military advisers increased to 21,000 and when a Vietcong mortar attack on

101   Saigon, March 1965. After the attack on the U.S. Embassy.   102   Saigon, June 1965.
The execution of a Vietcong terrorist.   103   South Vietnamese troops with parents (the
father a Vietcong suspect) and their dead child.   104   Khe Sanh, February 1968.
American marines rush a wounded comrade to a helicopter.   105   Mekong Delta, January
1967. An American soldier leads captured and blindfolded Vietcong.   106   Hué, February
1968. Men of the U.S. 1st Air Cavalry drag a wounded comrade to safety after a Vietcong
ambush.   107   Danang, January 1969. A captured Vietcong gets a drink.
108   Saigon, May 1968. Refugees from the Vietcong offensive on their way to a refugee
centre.   109   Phu Bai, March 1968. The U.S. 1st Cavalry runs for cover after a rocket hits
the airstrip

the Bien Hoa air base on 1 November destroyed 27 U.S. planes and helicopters, American Congressmen began to join the Saigon government in dangerous demands to extend the war to North Vietnam on Communist China's doorstep.

In February a Vietcong attack on the Pleiku air base destroyed or damaged another 20 aircraft and killed eight Americans. This provided the excuse that America needed to 'escalate' the war. On 7 February another reprisal air raid was made and from 2 March U.S. planes began systematic round-the-clock bombing of strategic targets in North Vietnam, flying an average of 70 sorties a day. These retaliatory strikes were intended not only to boost sagging South Vietnamese morale but to force North Vietnam to end its assistance to the Vietcong and negotiate.

Vietcong terrorism, however, increased, culminating in an attack on 30 March on the American embassy in Saigon itself, in which 22 Americans and Vietnamese were killed. It was obvious that South Vietnam could no longer be defended without a direct occupation by U.S. troops. On 8 March 3,500 marines landed at the air base at Danang, and by Christmas 1965 there were 190,000 U.S. troops in Vietnam. America's role had ceased to be advisory and instead her participation had become direct. What had been a regional conflict had become a world problem. Now that she was fully committed and had announced her intention to stop a Communist victory the United States could not afford to draw back. Danger of the conflict spreading was obviously great. The Vietcong immediately threatened to invite the aid of 'foreign volunteers' and China promised she would not stand by if North Vietnam was invaded. While military and economic aid flowed from China into North Vietnam the Chinese loudly demanded that Russia should take concrete military action to aid the North Vietnamese. Russian aid was limited to surface-to-air missiles and jets as defence against American bombing, but two American bombers shot down in July and August by Soviet-manned missile launchers were a timely reminder of the possibility of a direct clash between the super-powers.

The increased number of U.S. troops, reinforced by 15,000 South Koreans and 2,000 New Zealanders, enabled operations against the Vietcong to become more offensive. A large-scale 'search and destroy' policy was launched in the jungles, and an attempt was made to draw the Vietcong into open conventional warfare in which they could be destroyed. One entire Vietcong regiment was wiped out in this fashion but at the close of the year it was still estimated that Vietcong strength was over 200,000, including 15,000 North Vietnamese regulars who had infiltrated into the Central Highlands of South Vietnam. While America would consider only the complete withdrawal of the Vietcong from South Vietnam, the North Vietnamese, despite the continued bombing, showed no signs of giving way. After a 37-day pause to allow them to reconsider, bombing was resumed on 31 January 1966. By 20 April three times more bombs were falling per month on North Vietnam than had been dropped in the Korean war, and more than had been dropped on Europe in World War II. On 12 April 1,400,000 lbs of explosive fell alone on the Muggia Pass, one of the principal supply routes from North Vietnam to Laos, and the tempo of the bombing increased throughout the summer and autumn. In theory it was still limited to strategic targets, but in practice it brought heavy civilian casualties and widespread devastation to houses, hospitals, and schools, which aroused angry criticism from Western and neutral opinion. North Vietnamese complaints were supported by the reports of Western journalists. A French newspaperman visiting the town of Phuly in December 1966 wrote:

. . . I could see only shreds of walls, piles of broken branches and twisted metal, bomb craters, broken pylons, and houses which were . . . blasted and uninhabitable. Phuly is dead; the final blow was struck on 2 October 1966 and the aircraft came back on October 3 and 9. . . . It was no doubt difficult to destroy the railway installations without destroying the town. . . .[1]

While the North Vietnamese constructed thousands of concrete manhole shelters with 2-inch-thick covers, in the South the greatly reinforced American troops used their massive weight of numbers and equipment in large-scale offensives to harry the Vietcong and North Vietnamese, while ARVN was left to pacify the countryside. As the Americans attempted to drive the Vietcong from their jungle hideouts and village bases the war grew more brutal. Torture of prisoners was already commonplace, and as South Vietnamese methods of interrogation became known Western opinion was again disturbed. With Vietcong supplies reduced by the bombing, Americans at the close of the year were optimistic but no clear progress had been made. Vietcong who had been cleared from an area swiftly infiltrated back when the Americans left. Between January and March, for example, the U.S. carried out a massive clearing operation at Bong Son which they claimed had freed 140,000 people from Vietcong control. Within five days of their departure, however, the Vietcong were back in command. Elsewhere, forewarned by their intelligence, they melted away before American traps could be sprung, and the Americans began to experience the same frustration and bewilderment as the French had done before.

North Vietnamese were infiltrating into South Vietnam at the rate of 4,500 a month along the Ho Chi Minh Trail, which had been ingeniously camouflaged for 30 miles with a ceiling of bamboo and foliage (see Map 11). In contrast the South Vietnamese forces were of varying quality. 109,000 deserted during 1966 and many refused to patrol at night when the Vietcong took over in many areas. The guerrillas, indistinct from the local population, who gave them much support, were able to penetrate anywhere, as they showed on 13 April 1966 when they mortared Saigon air base, destroying 33 planes. In January 1967 15,000 U.S. and ARVN troops cleared 60 square miles of forest north-west of Saigon which had sheltered guerrillas for 20 years. The area was honeycombed with bunkers and escape tunnels, living, storage, and hospital quarters. When the operation ended on 26 January the villages concerned had been burned, bombed, or bulldozed and 6,000 peasants were homeless. 1,400 Vietcong had been killed or captured but by 2 February they were back.

Baffled by their failure to secure a victory despite their enormous superiority in firepower and equipment, the Americans brought into use a whole series of new weapons and techniques of warfare which caused the U.N. Secretary-General, U Thant, to describe the Vietnam war as 'the most barbarous in history'. A new adhesive napalm which clung to the skin inflicting horrible burns, 'non-lethal' gases, phosphorus bombs, and anti-personnel bombs which shot thousands of steel pellets, brought increasing world criticism of American involvement in Vietnam. In an attempt to stop North Vietnamese aid through the demilitarised zone on the 17th parallel, defoliants were sprayed on the jungle to destroy the vegetation and reveal the supply lines. After a 12-day battle in the spring of 1967 U.S. marines seized Khe Sanh, which controlled the routes leading from North Vietnam to the South through Laos. 1,100 Vietcong were killed. On three other occasions when the Vietcong attacked in strength they were

[1] Keesing's Contemporary Archives, p. 22571.

again defeated with heavy losses but there was no sign that their resistance was wilting. Hanoi and Haiphong were bombed for the first time on 29 June as restrictions were lifted on many target areas. Large portions of the latter and 85 per cent of North Vietnam's power stations were destroyed, but the North Vietnamese, accustomed to hardship and death, still resisted, believing that sooner or later American will would collapse as that of the French had done.

By mid-November 1967 470,000 American troops were committed to Vietnam – more than had been employed in the Korean war. 35,000 more were in Thailand, mounting from the huge base at Sattahip Bay the massive air strikes which previously had come from Guam 2,500 miles away. The Americans were supported by 645,000 South Vietnamese, 46,000 South Koreans, and contingents from Australia, Thailand, the Philippines, and New Zealand. Major parts of the 7th Fleet were operating off the North Vietnamese coast. Since 1961 17,000 American troops had been killed and 90,000 wounded, making Vietnam the fifth most costly war in American history. 60,000 South Vietnamese were also dead. Yet little had been achieved. Two and a half years of bombing had done untold damage, but with North Vietnamese regulars keeping open the Ho Chi Minh Trail the Vietcong, despite 200,000 dead, were stronger than when the war began. They controlled 40 per cent of South Vietnam as compared with 51 per cent a year before, but only one of the country's 44 provinces was completely free from guerrillas. Colossal Russian and Chinese aid had supplied the Vietcong with the most modern weapons. It had also provided North Vietnam with 8,000 anti-aircraft guns and 50 missile sites which had shot down 1,300 U.S. planes while a further 1,500 had been lost through accidents in a difficult terrain.

Bitterly criticised by even her NATO allies for her conduct of a war which was costing her £3,000 a second, and in which her young men were beginning to refuse to fight, America found herself in a hopeless dilemma. To prevent Chinese expansion and nuclear blackmail in South-East Asia America had to stay in South Vietnam where she had no moral right to be and was supporting a hopelessly unpopular régime. She had the power to wipe out North Vietnam overnight, but if North Vietnam was invaded China would intervene, the Soviet-American *détente* would collapse, and nuclear war might result. The longer the war continued the greater grew American unpopularity abroad and demands at home for drastic action to end the drain of men and money. While America would only stop the bombing if North Vietnamese infiltration ceased, Hanoi would not negotiate until the bombing ended. In November 1967 the U.S. commander, General Westmoreland, optimistically forecast that his 'search and destroy' operations would enable American troops to withdraw in two years, but other officials spoke gloomily of stalemate.

Westmoreland's hopes of conclusive victory were crushed by a massive Vietcong offensive in the first two months of 1968. On 3 January a rocket bombardment of Danang air base and raids on many other small towns and bases were a sign of things to come. By 21 January 4,000 marines at the U.S. base and airstrip of Khe Sanh, 6 miles from the Laotian border, were isolated and besieged by 25,000 North Vietnamese. Khe Sanh had been intended to stop enemy infiltration and to prevent the Communist troops from marching southward upon Saigon. All civilians were evacuated and reinforcements and supplies were flown in for a long siege. Although fog hindered flying, all missions against North Vietnam were cancelled and massive air strikes against the besiegers began.

In alarm at the build-up of Communist forces the Americans on 29 January cancelled a truce for the New Year Tet holiday. Next day the Vietcong launched their biggest offensive of the war, attacking 30 of the 44 provincial capitals, and American bases and installations throughout South Vietnam. Within a few days they had been driven from most places, but in Saigon and the Buddhist city of Hué bitter fighting raged until 23 and 24 February respectively. Between 29–31 January 5,000 guerrillas infiltrated on scooters, buses, and lorries into Saigon unnoticed among the many visitors for the Tet holiday. Armed and aided by the Vietcong underground, at 3.00 a.m. on 31 January suicide squads attacked the Presidential Palace, Saigon Radio Station, and the American billets and embassy. Others attacked the airport and occupied the working-class section of the city where they armed their many supporters. As martial law was declared U.S. tanks and infantry rushed to Saigon and an American general took command. Savage fighting ensued in streets packed with refugees in which the Americans used tanks, armoured cars, and mortars. Vietcong prisoners were shot on the spot by South Vietnamese police and troops, while housing blocks held by the Vietcong were bombed and machine-gunned by planes and helicopters. The city was finally cleared by 23 February, but it still remained threatened by guerrilla activity in June.

At the same time on 31 January the Vietcong had overwhelmed the main government positions in the old imperial capital of Hué. The battle for its recapture lasted three weeks. Marines retook the new portion of the city on 10 February after losing a quarter of their number. Only when the citadel across the Perfume river had been enveloped by bombs, rockets, napalm, and nausea gas, and shelled by the 7th Fleet, was it stormed on 24 February. Its surviving defenders melted into the night, leaving behind the corpses of a thousand civilians who had been executed during the occupation.

While Vietcong hopes of a general uprising had failed through insufficient popular support the Tet offensive defeated the American struggle for 'the hearts and minds' of the people. It showed that no place was safe from the Vietcong terrorism, and that the Americans could guarantee the safety of no pacified area. With insufficient troops to hold both town and countryside the policy of 'search and destroy' was abandoned. Soldiers were withdrawn from the jungles to protect the towns, and the rural areas reverted to the Vietcong. The Americans were back to the position of 1965, except that their problems were complicated by thousands of homeless refugees bringing in their wake cholera, typhoid, and bubonic plague.

Grave anxiety still existed about the fate of Khe Sanh. The similarities to Dien Bien Phu were too close for comfort. The marine base was situated in a bowl in the hills open to artillery and rocket fire, and it was rumoured that Giap himself was directing the siege. On 7 February the outlying Special Forces Camp at Lang Vei was taken by tanks; the airstrip became unusable and a major assault was only repulsed after a 61-hour battle. Nuclear weapons were suggested as a means of relief, but Khe Sanh did not become another Dien Bien Phu. While giant B.52s maintained 'the most concentrated aerial bombardment in history' against the besiegers, who were only 100 yards away, a 3,000-strong relief force launched a drive overland. After two months the siege was lifted, but the base was abandoned in June 1968.

An incident on the night of 22–23 January had emphasised how easily the situation in South-East Asia could escalate into nuclear war when the *Pueblo*, a U.S. electronic spy ship, was seized by North Korean gunboats and taken into Wonsan. The Americans claimed the *Pueblo* was in international waters and labelled her seizure an act of war. As angry Congressmen demanded that force should be used to secure the ship's release, reservists were called up and the nuclear aircraft-carrier *Enterprise*, the world's largest warship, moved with support ships towards Wonsan. Russia was bound by treaty to protect North Korea if she was attacked. Kosygin, dismissing the incident as 'unimportant', wisely called for steps to cool the crisis down. America was temporarily humiliated by another small nation but she was not anxious for a further war. The rising cost of the Vietnam war was partly responsible for a serious American gold crisis in March 1968 and after secret meetings between U.S. and North Vietnamese representatives President Johnson ordered on 31 March all naval and air attacks to cease except those below the 20th parallel where the build-up of North Vietnamese troops occurred. Three days later America and North Vietnam agreed to begin peace talks in Paris the following month while the war in South Vietnam ground on. Early exchanges in the talks suggested that they would, like the Korean negotiations, take a long time, and even a complete American halt in the bombing at the end of October brought little headway.

Russia, unlike China, had long favoured negotiations over Vietnam. She, like America, had realised that neither could attack the other without being destroyed in retaliation. By 1968 America possessed 1,054 I.C.B.M.s situated underground, plus 656 missiles in 41 Polaris submarines. She also had 520 inter-continental bombers with 4,000 nuclear warheads. In contrast Russia possessed 720 I.C.B.M.s, 130 submarine missiles, and 150 inter-continental bombers with 1,000 warheads. Russia's armoury also included 725 medium-range missiles capable of striking European and Asian targets. While America had the numerical superiority in I.C.B.M.s, many of Russia's missiles were more powerful. American experts calculated that if Russia delivered her entire missile force at the American strategic forces, keeping her refire missiles and bomber-delivered nuclear weapons for the American cities, half America's missiles would survive to destroy Russia. In the same way Russia could withstand a first strike by America and inflict crippling damage in return. A number of Russia's cities and bases were protected by a Ballistic Missile Defence System whereby long-range radar detected incoming

110   The crew of the *Pueblo* taken prisoner by the North Koreans

missiles and released counter-missiles to meet them, but American scientists had developed an I.C.B.M. with multiple warheads which would penetrate this system. Russian scientists had produced a nuclear weapon that could be put into orbit round the earth and directed down to its target, but American over-the-horizon radar would give ample warning of its approach.

That the nuclear stalemate was accompanied in Europe by a political stalemate was revealed by the Russian occupation of Czechoslovakia in August 1968. Here the more liberal régime of Alexander Dubcek, who had replaced the tough Stalinist Novotny in January, threatened a Czech withdrawal from the Warsaw Pact and closer ties with the West. If this happened Russia's defensive barrier would be split, and she would again face military danger from West Germany. On the night of 20 August half a million troops from Russia, Poland, East Germany, Hungary, and Bulgaria occupied 'the dagger pointing at the heart of Russia' in a brilliantly executed military operation. Western verbal protests were strong. A NATO warning against similar invasions was issued to Russia on 16 November. NATO forces in West Germany were strengthened, but the unfortunate Czechs, who could only offer passive resistance, were inevitably left like the Hungarians to their fate. The best hope for peace lay in a stable balance of power which the Czechs were unbalancing. If they had been allowed to take greater freedom Romania and other satellites would have followed and Russia may have been forced into more widespread military action resulting in war.

In September 1967 America significantly decided not to install a Ballistic Missile Defence System against Russia since her ability to absorb a 'first strike' and retaliate was the best deterrent. She decided, however, to install a limited Ballistic Missile Defence System against China, who in October 1966 had produced her first guided missile, and in June 1967 had exploded her first hydrogen bomb. Chinese nuclear development had been severely checked during 1966–7 by serious internal disturbances which amounted almost to civil war, resulting from an attempt by Mao Tse-Tung to purge the party leadership and produce a new classless society. By the early 1970s, however, experts calculated China would have a stockpile of nuclear weapons and the rockets to deliver them. An agreement with Albania in December 1968 gave her the possibility of a missile base in Europe which would threaten not only Western Europe but also European Russia.

> If an atomic war was fought [Mao Tse-Tung told a Western journalist] and half of mankind died the other half would remain . . . imperialism would be razed to the ground and the whole world would become socialist; in a number of years there would be 2,700 million people again. . . .

Scientists putting their findings upon nuclear war before the United Nations in October 1967 did not agree that even the massive Chinese population could survive such a calamity.

> . . . Were such weapons ever to be used [they stated] hundreds of millions of people might be killed and civilisation as we know it would . . . come to an end. . . . Those who survived the immediate destruction . . . would be exposed to widely-spreading radio-active contamination. . . . [The arms race has] resulted in the production of weapons whose destructive power is more than sufficient to eliminate all mankind. . . .[1]

[1] Keesing's Contemporary Archives, p. 22388.

111   Bratislava, August 1968. Slovaks and Czechs surround Russian tanks to protest against the Soviet occupation

ACKNOWLEDGEMENTS

THE AUTHOR AND PUBLISHERS wish to record their grateful thanks to copyright owners for the use of the illustrations listed below:

The Associated Press Ltd for: 5, 20, 24, 44, 48, 78, 89, 95, 99, 104, 110
Barnaby's Picture Library for: 23
Camera Press Ltd for: 10, 15, 16, 29, 35, 37, 53, 54, 77, 97
Imperial War Museum for: 30
Israeli Embassy, London for: 75, 76
Keystone Press Agency Ltd for: 31, 32, 33, 34, 36, 73
Erich Lessing and the John Hillelson Agency Ltd for: 72
Novosti Press Agency for: 6, 7, 62
Pictorial Press Ltd for: 4, 8, 21, 22
Paul Popper Ltd for: 11, 41, 47, 50, 57, 58, 60, 63, 65, 66, 74, 86, 93
Press Information Bureau, Government of India, New Delhi for: 94
Radio Times Hulton Picture Library for: title-page, 2, 17, 18, 27, 38, 39, 40, 42, 43, 45, 46, 55, 69, 70
Süddeutscher Verlag, Bild-Archiv, Munich for: 68
Times Publishing, Sendirian Berhad, Kuala Lumpur for: 56
United Press International (UK) Ltd for: 1, 3, 12, 13, 25, 26, 28, 49, 51, 52, 59, 61, 64, 67, 79, 80, 81, 82, 83, 84, 85, 87, 88, 90, 91, 92, 96, 98, 100, 101, 102, 103, 105, 106, 107, 108, 109, 111
United States Information Service for: 9, 14

and for Quotations:

Keesing's Contemporary Archives
Macmillan and Co. Ltd for the extracts from *Korea: The Limited War* by D. Rees

Index

Printed in Great Britain by Jarrold & Sons Limited, Norwich